Past
Present and
Future in
Poetry

Robert Stevens

Arranged by

Abbie Stevens

Grosvenor House
Publishing Limited

This book is published by
Grosvenor House Publishing Ltd
Link House
140 The Broadway, Tolworth, Surrey, KT6 7HT.
www.grosvenorhousepublishing.co.uk

A CIP record for this book
is available from the British Library

ISBN 978-1-83975-808-9

Many thanks to my Mum and Dad
They where pure gold

Abbie took my thoughts
As page by page it grew

We did the impossible to bring this to you

CONTENTS

HOME LIVERPOOL 1936

Long ago at Christmas
and when I was a boy
then I used to wonder
maybe I'd get a toy

Dad crippled World War One
four kids too young to work
dads pension just nine bob
put parish in mums purse

We had gas for cooking
and used two small gas rings
coal far too expensive
old papers cooked most things

Sisters gathered papers
just every where they could
when burnt they kept us warm
and cooked our food quite good

But no one had a watch
just one alarm clock there
high up oh the mantle
ticking away the year

I guess toys don't matter
have food and shelter here
it was home where we lived
with mum dad to care

And yes it was Christmas
no gifts or cards to share
but we had each other
mum and dad was there

KELLY'S POEM

It's goodbye Kelly
we all have to go
fate makes his mind up
and we can't say no
life had its good times
and you know the bad
good to be with you
you enjoy your world
horses and haircuts
and fun with the girls
your always busy
live life on the run
know South Africa
and Rhodesian sun
Chutney your kitten
as black as the night
sleeps where you laid him
so just say good night

Dad

OUR SUSIE

Our Susie a quiet girl
not catch her in a whirl
helps at home now and then
or she's upstairs reading
in her back bedroom den
and she can bake a cake
do a roast no mistake
and if your lucky
you may just catch a smile
find her on winters night
curled up in firelight
deep in an old armchair
Susie's happy and at home
the worlds outside not here

Love Dad

SUSIE

Our Susie hard to know
Not often say hello
in her world seems alone
loved by all when at home

Seems good times pass her by
all she'll give is a sigh
comfy in old armchair
don't want to go out there

And the last few years
we have all shed some tears
guess you have done your best
just relax a well earned rest

God Bless - Dad

HAPPY MEMORIES

Looking back to days of old
Love and laughter tears untold
I miss the country and open fields
Those hay bale rides with squeaky wheels

Warm log fires and family nights
Dads apple pies a glorious sight
The smell of coffee and fresh bread
Home grown fruit in a bowl of red

Frightening storms that look like a maize
Warm winter and scorching summer days
Riding bareback to the lakeside
Long standing friendships talking old times

By Kelly Stevens – 31/05/1962 – 25/11/2018

HOME

Over mantle
in our bedroom
double the light
and chased the gloom

Curtains we had
and just afford
and no lino
on floorboard

Bed was cosy
and this was home
and none of us
ever alone

We had a sheet
and bolster too
army blankets
mum had washed through

The candles gleam
on mantle wall
this was the thirties
I do recall

YESTERDAY 1937

I do remember yesterday
when we had time to talk and play
of all the things we never had
sometimes happy and often sad

The holidays we never went
presents we never got or sent
our Christmases were all the same
there was no one that we could blame

Everyone knew that we were poor
and in the thirty's thousands more
found poverty was hard to beat
in Liverpool down every street

MERSEY MOON

Moonlight on the Mersey
romantic it can be
when the one you care for
is staring out to sea

And soon she will travel
far out across that sea
only a memory
of love will stay with me

Travel is her business
she does it very well
will we stay together
guess only time will tell

POVERTY 1936

As a boy I walked the street
never shoes upon my feet
pennies few and far between
hard times known and often seen

A lot more dinner times than dinner
I must have been from average thinner
huddled up in bed at night
with my two sisters snug and tight

Christmas carols we would sing
but Santa never brought a thing
we never ever found out why
each Christmas Eve he passed us by

Father ill upon his bed
injured in the war mum said
nine bob pension all he got
so parish handouts was our lot

Good times I had and never cared
for richer folk or how they fared
yet sometimes I did think it wrong
that we were poor so very long

HOME LIVERPOOL 1930'S

It's true Mum and dad
tried very hard
to bring up four kids
on a PAC card

Our dad was injured
in the First World War
nine bob war pension
was all that he saw

Arthur and Edith
plus our Liz and me
we struggled along
as best as could be

We lived in hard times
and money was short
but we all got by
with a little thought

So our food and rent
they were number one
holidays Christmas
they were just not on

MIDNIGHT CALLS

Sometimes at night
knock on the door
in early hours
PAC Chore

Civilian and
a policeman there
check you are you
and who else there

Go through the house
wake all folk up
and only then
our front door shut

They check all homes
to see you there
lots on parish
everywhere

LIVERPOOL 1934

On the street I lived
people very poor
easy to find out
knock on any door

Lots of things missing
food and comfort too
cash very little
got what you were due

Holidays Christmas
never on your list
warm clothes in winter
these you really missed

All things got used to
poverty and poor
at home Liverpool
nineteen thirty four

PAC help you
enough to get by
trying to stretch it
brought tears to the eye

MUM

Could make a meal
six pence of bones
how she did it
God only knows

Just lots of veg
go in the pot
boil three hours
it feed us lot

So Saturday night
the pot goes on
Sunday morning
the dripping done

Skim this off pot
nice spread you've got
will go on toast
for all us lot

GARDEN STREET NUMBER 24

Smithdown Lane is not the same
the houses have all gone
where are the shops and grocers
the school where I was from?

At Garden Street number twenty four
I spent my early youth
alas there were no gardens
and that's the honest truth

Houses marching up a hill
like soldiers back to back
side by side with cellars
and everything they lack

No hot water bathrooms
and no electric light
we lived in the cellars
the toilets are out the back

But this is just a memory
and pictures in the mind
the bad times are forgotten
and good times silver lined

GARDEN STREET 1936

Garden Street made our home
six of us not alone
twenty four on our door
we could not ask for more

Our street full of families
and many unemployed
they did the best they could
but no one overjoyed

Looking around our new place
found just a street away
my favourite place the pics
Liz take me there Saturday

Kids in street a mixed lot
and all go to our school
mostly hard up like us
but friendly as a rule

Went to pics Saturday
and Shirley Temple on
golden curls and big blue eyes
and my heart simply spun

THIRTIES 1936

I lived in the thirties
aged seven I was there
poverty was normal
and we all had our share

It was hard to get by
and families by the score
helped out by the parish
knew then that they were poor

We just about made it
for six of us to feed
and mum never failed us
a miracle indeed

Dad a wounded soldier
a small pension his
splashed out on a Friday night
two fags and matches bliss

Never any problems
this was our normal life
something you got used to
and nothing else in sight

24 GARDEN STREET – LIFE AT HOME
(1936-1937)

As a child I never thought
of all the things we never bought
we had so little in home
even a chair feel alone
we had two tables as well
and an armchair for Dad
also a long black dresser
this had dishes and crockery
and even clothes in
had a standing cupboard
purported metal down sides
it had shelves for food
stone floor cool in summer
chilly in winter alas no carpet
or lino we hoped to make a rug
a good cooking range we never used
coal too dear collected old
newspapers could cook and get warm
burning them had no gas cooker
just two small gas rings
a gas light in the cellar
no electric lighting in street at all

Dad was crippled in the war
and unable to work
he got a small war pension
of nine shillings a week
we got assistance from local
parish funds
Christmas, Easter hols
we could not afford so got to miss
dad like a smoke so pension day
I'd go to the corner shop
two fags and some matches cost a penny
wrapped up in newspaper
dads treat
Mum ran the family no fuss
did the impossible
make a meal out of nothing
thousands like us
poverty no stranger

MUM AND DAD LIVERPOOL 1936

Never write of parents
for they're no longer here
yet they brought up four kids
miracle that was clear

Dad not use his right side
paralysed in the war
nine bob weekly pension
and that was all he saw

Mum got some assistance
and that from PAC
about two quid I think
to fend off poverty

Furniture we had some
dresser table and chairs
small gas rings to cook on
where we all lived downstairs

We lived in the cellar
a cooking range was there
we had no coal for fire
we burnt newspapers there

Coal was too expensive
need pennies for the gas
papers very useful
they made our money last

Older sisters find them
for most are thrown away
we cooked throughout winter
with papers every day

Holidays we had none
and Christmas just the same
birthdays no different
but none of us complained

So what you've never had
you never really missed
mum and dad were special
now them we would have missed

MY CHILDHOOD PAST 1939

Our train has stopped
Rossett North Wales
tiny village
it's in Welsh Wales

Then cups of tea
and cakes galore
we all well served
could eat no more

All kids spread out
sixty or more
into new homes
till end of war

So our future
now it brand new
and none of us
would have a clue

LIVERPOOL MARKET 1937

It's Saturday
we go to town
for fish and meat
the price is down

Back of market
it auctioned off
so fish and meat
take quite a drop

There's plaice and cod
and conger eel
all expensive
but here a steal

A piece of meat
we also got
so late tonight
it into pot

Two fish boxes
we take away
will keep our fire
alight all day

LIVERPOOL UNIS

Good place to be from
so well known abroad
but it is changing
the scousers have scored

A teaching city
students from abroad
would be a pity
if scousers ignored

Unis are busy
and builders too
putting the pool back
on the leading track

PENALLY

A chapel in the valley
in sight of the sea
quiet and forgotten
they call it Penally

The graves are few in number
and seem to huddle close
as in the distance thunder
echoes along the coast

Winter storms will come and go
and summer suns caress
this little graveyard by the sea
where memories can rest

24 GARDEN STREET

Last house on the right
at top of street
live in the cellar
to share the heat

A cooking range
we never use
old newspapers
they cook our food

Coal was too dear
newspapers free
they light your fire
in poverty

The cellar floor
was paving stone
rugs and lino
not in our home

Table chest chairs
an old armchair
and only dad
could relax there

GLOUCESTER PLACE

Old tumbledown town where I was born
a place to love a place to mourn
a place to live and a place to die
now broken buildings reach for the sky

When I was a child here I would roam
barefoot and ragged but never alone
for friends were many and troubles few
folks were so kindly they stood by you

Old tumbledown town your streets are bare
your doorways broken your windows stare
as they gaze down they seem to sigh
my heart is heavy I could almost cry

I guess it's the end they'll have their way
they say you're condemned you've had your day
and now I hear bulldozers roar
step into my heart forever more

BONFIRE NIGHT

Fifth of November   25
when I was a kid
definitely scares you
big bonfires did

They lit them early
and the flames leapt high
and they're lighting up
a November sky

The noise and racket
creates quite a din
and we sometimes called
the firemen in

The heat cracked windows
and blistered door paint
firemen cooled it down
and got some restraint

But no one complained
only one a year
a massive bonfire
we'll remember here

OUR HOUSE 1936

There were no gardens
in our Garden street
twenty four houses
with cellars beneath

They stand side by side
they march up a hill
homes for the families
a future they fill

And not gardens here
just no room at all
but all of us have
our own backyard wall

So bright and lively
the colours will call
all decorated
their own backyard wall

CANDLES 1935

Candles showed the way
with us every day
lightened up our lives
chased the gloom away

Winter evenings dark
up and down the stairs
light up a candle
then you have no fears

Not got electric
Candles everywhere
they show us to bed
have no gaslight there

Only in cellar
gas on mantle there
pennies in meter
light up everywhere

Shilling a dozen
so a penny each
lighted up our world
that quite often bleak

NO WORK

Sometimes life a mountain
you climb and get nowhere
many years you struggle
the peak is just not there

Trouble can slow you down
and it increase the mist
work can be hard to find
and many chances missed

But got to keep trying
and luck will come your way
at last a wage packet
then time for hip-hip-hooray

JUST CHRISTMAS

Christmas round the corner
and snowflakes in the air
I hear children singing
their carols everywhere

Shops are full of people
for Father Christmas here
busy in his grotto
with many children there

Special time is Christmas
with gently falling snow
all recall the first one
that one from long ago

MY STORY LIVERPOOL 1936

We all have a story
and sometimes it gets told
but memory is there
so it can then unfold

I was born in the thirties
well nineteen twenty nine
we lived in Liverpool
that was poverty time

Dad a wounded soldier
but injured right hand side
cannot earn a living
it could have hurt his pride

He married had four kids
and me the youngest son
parish and a pension
was two pounds twenty one

We all somehow got by
for mum was good at meals
bones from the butchers shop
and veg to make the meal

Christmas came, Christmas went
and stockings we'd hang up
mum filled them with fruit
Santa never showed up

Mum dad and us four kids
got through another year
maybe in the future
the good times would appear

WHERE ARE THEY LIVERPOOL 1936

Hot summers we knew
noisy tramcars too

Blazing bonfire nights
river Mersey sights

Ferries to and fro
and the Lord Mayors show

Illuminated tram
if can get on

Work still hard to get
things won't change just yet

We all struggle by
and all wonder why

Some things never change
will future rearrange

ONE LAST TRIP

Cemetery in winter
and no one want to know
everyone is sleeping
with it's blanket of snow

Everyone is someone
the young and the old no doubt
and one day we'll join them
that's when our team runs out

NO CHRISTMAS

Christmas was stolen
nowhere to be found
and taken away
with never a sound

No sign of the tree
decorations none
coloured lights gone
a fairy just one

Puzzled who took it
could be Christmas past
now they're together
together at last

FOR CHRISTMAS

Do it today
for tomorrow
too far away
you may forget
that special card
someone waiting
that can be hard
Christmas
it's once a year
so don't forget
and stop that tear
sure to return
in your new year

US AT HOME 1936

It was a zone
that we called home
back street of town
we settled down

The times were hard
our family poor
we just got by
like many more

Parish helped us
and Dad not work
injured soldier
small pension perk

So Mum and Dad
and four kids too
all made their way
as they had to

Few possessions
no carpets there
had no lino
on floor or stair

We bought no coal
for it too dear
newspapers free
gave warmth and cheer

Food a problem
from butcher bones
a load of veg
this satisfy six hungry mouths

Warm clothes needed
second hand true
you patch and wash
they see you through

Arthur Edie
our Liz and me
all got used to
the poverty

A WINTERS NIGHT 1937

A winters night
in Liverpool
the street lamps lit
provide a pool
of yellow light
just here and there
on this cold night
and family's here
they settle down
another night
their hardships fight
and few at work
no jobs to get
parish will help
but only just
so struggle you must
we just get by
because we must
and our future
is just the same
for poverty
is not a game

JUST CHRISTMAS 1938

Christmas once again
coloured lights aflame

A massive tree there
where in Clayton Square

Center of city
it's all free to see

Shops bursting with life
the cold like a knife

Christmas in the air
carols everywhere

Where's the falling snow
kids all want to know

This a special time
almost Auld Lang Syne

CHRISTMAS WHERE

Christmas a long way off
I heard it say goodbye
It's coloured lights twinkled
in a darkening sky

I watched in starlight
was searching high and low
just heading for the east
where it was told to go

Will it ever come back
alas its hard to know
disappeared in stardust
and not much I could do

One day we will find it
and bring it safe back home
till then there's no Christmas
till then I am alone

CHRISTMAS

Just a thought for Christmas
from me to you I'll send
hoping Yuletide brings to you
the love and joy that lends
itself to all who seek it
that knows no barrier
the kind that led wise men of old
to that first distant star

I may not often see you
or write you every day
but at this time you're in my thoughts
in a very special way
no matter where you wander
no matter where you roam
old friends and new still there for you
where the sign says home sweet home

There is a Christmas Spirit
and a Christmas cheer
these things I wish to send you
because I hold you dear
but if we were together
no place I'd rather be
I wish you a Merry Christmas
sincere and tenderly

THE CHRISTMAS SPIRIT

On Christmas Eve I walked the streets
that round a city ran
and wondered if the Christmas Spirit
and been found by man
I looked in many faces
questioned everyone
and searched in many places
for the spirit that was gone
some were sober on their feet
some lay on the ground
I then began to wonder
if it ever would be found
I visited cathedrals
and many a church pew
sang with them their Christmas songs
sang their carols too
They were reverent to their God
sincerely did they sing
but the Christmas Spirit was not there
I left to find this thing
beyond the church through falling snow
stumbled a woman I seemed to know
she clutched a baby to her breast
here indeed an ended quest
the woman laughed in mild surprise
but I saw a God in a baby's eyes

MUM 1935

Mum number one
without a doubt
never ever
hear her shout

Always ready
always there
sure and able
she would be fair

And sometimes Dad
might swear a bit
she would not hear
or have a fit

She's got control
ad guides us all
will lift us up
if down we fall

Just veg and bones
may not appeal
give them to mum
she'll make a meal

We all think Dads
a lucky guy
if you knew mum
you'd not ask why

FOOD COUPONS

Alas one day
Mum lost her purse
made her money
fifteen bob worse

We had to go
and ask for more
at Brougham house
and knock on door

I went with Mum
an office there
we sat outside
on old oak chair

Then they called us
to great big room
many people
I see through gloom

Mum told them when
she lost her cash
many nodded
and questions asked

After two hours
we told to wait
so we sat down
to hear our fate

But food coupons
were all we got
each half inch square
but we need the lot

Essentials just
to help us out
luxuries no
can do without

Embarrassing
to shop like this
but poverty
cannot be bliss

DAD 1935

Dad a soldier
fought in the war
four years of hell
you can be sure

Half his body
that had cost him
he cannot work
took on the chin

But Wed he got
and fathered four
our Mum and Dad
extremely poor

Small war pension
was all he got
he wanted work
but he could not

A tough cockney
he six feet tall
no invalid
he answered call

But Dad was Dad
for family care
swear like a trouper
but always there

MERSEY MERSEY

Mersey Mersey
pity on me
you took my girl
went off to sea

Liver birds said
it made their day
for river to
misbehave thus way

True I worry
that' has been said
she only go
to Birkenhead

CHILDREN

Children are special
have no enemies
even a baby
will smile just to please

As they grow older
and play in the street
no ones a stranger
and all they will greet

New world exciting
and that's to be sure
till they leave childhood
and open life's door

HEAVY HORSE PARADE 1936

Great shire horses
the council used
pulling trailers
household refuse

One day a week
in Garden Street
these huge horses
us kids would greet

But they do have
a special day
are on parade
the first of May

Council staff there
comb horses hair
have bright brass shining
on May Day

There's crowds around
horses line up
the Lord Major
will do his stuff

The winner picked
the crowd shout loud
I think horses
were very proud.

CHRISTMAS 1936

I see it's Christmas
gently falling snow
hear children singing
carols that I know

Everyone busy
Christmas trees alight
shops full of people
Christmas Eve tonight

As a boy wondered
about Santa Claus
not get down chimneys
he must knock at doors

Me and two sisters
slept behind front door
we slept there all night
Santa never saw

Well maybe next year
have Christmas tree
decorate it
for family

Gently snow falls
street windows lit up
Still hear the carols
Mum comes tuck us up

EVACUEE

Sometimes if your lucky
you will stay in one home
then they have to move you
it's then you feel alone

About sixty of us
and all from Liverpool
all of us caught scabies
so hospital the rule

About three weeks later
a children's home for me
it also in Wrexham
a massive family

This time sent to a farm
with lots of cows in view
think it was dairy farm
and always lots to do

Back to school in Rossett
almost a mile away
so I'm a paper boy
bike helps me every day

And I'm almost twelve
dad has died must go home
get job and help mum out
as mum and Liz alone

Funeral Saturday
so me and a milk truck ride
all the way Liverpool
the farmers wife decide

Hooray I'm home at last
too late no one is there
I have missed funeral
only time for the tears

SIS AND ME EVACUEES

Can you remember
third of September
then we were at war
no one knows what for

Just to the country
was where we must go
but how long that for
no one seems to know

Me and my sister
me ten she fourteen
are very puzzled
at what it might mean

Gas masks are tried on
but they are strange things
the big girls make bags
but with carry slings

They are to carry
clothes that we may need
few kids have cases
something never need

We never have hols
or they very rare
so case not needed
don't go anywhere

Sixty kids from school
gathered in the street
tears on young faces
this was not a treat

All bussed to station
teachers load the train
engine blows goodbye
when return again

LYTTON CINEMA

And two jam jars
if nice and clean
get me in free
see Lytton Screen

On Saturday
I'll go to pix
jam jars are cash
admission fix

Don't have much jam
so our bin bare
will have to go
seek jars elsewhere

Up and over
the backyard walls
some people shout
and lots of falls

But we got two
go pix again
that girl Shirley
what was her name

Doorman at desk
he's smart by far
checks carefully
my two jam jars

CHRISTMAS PAST

It's Christmas yes Christmas
and a cold frosty night
and all things you wanted
are just nowhere in sight

The good times and bad times
are all rolled into one
happy Christmas somewhere
yet I haven't seen one

Could be it stuck somewhere
and could have lost its way
it's just a memory
every Christmas Day

JUST US

Into the future
and headlong we go
no time for the past
we don't want to know

Those that we loved gone
are no longer here
the years have gone by
leave only a tear

They will remember
our kindness and care
and they won't forget
we were always there

POLICE CHARITY

Police charity
who help the poor
called me and Liz
inside their door

Mum took us up
and many there
so girls and boys
all get a share

Got shorts and shoes
green pullover
and underwear
but shoes not choose

For these were clogs
that no one wore
if you wore them
kids know your poor

But Liz looked great
in dress she choose
but like me too
she stick no shoes

BONFIRE NIGHT 1937

Bonfire night in Liverpool
lots of noise that is the rule
many streets with big bonfires
fantastic flames all desire

Lots of laughter lots of yells
fireman busy hear their bells
there's smoke and flames everywhere
it's bonfire night we don't care

Next year we'll do the same again
get the biggest highest flame
whole city must be alight
some bangers give me a fright

So my two sisters and me
see lots of fireworks for free
tomorrow we all turn up
clean the street and have a cup

ANY STREET 1936

Any street will be the same
sometimes wonder who to blame
once poverty gets a grip
our standard of life will slip

Money need to pay your way
Parish there to save the day
food and rent it will support
clothes and warmth it must abort

Winter puts the brake on food
a coal fire we must include
coal the cheapest heat we know
down the years we've found it so

True to say it was a fight
yet we lived and got it right
and none of us could be sure
what the future had in store

We lived that life day by day
could there be another way
maybe we could change that scene
only if we dream dream dream

CHRISTMAS WHEN

It will soon be Christmas
another year that's gone
the nights getting colder
a disappearing sun

Kids will have a good time
can't wait for Christmas Eve
wondering what presents
their likely to receive

Christmas my favourite
someone took it away
never did return it
it was a price to pay

Still hear the carols
and watch the falling snow
world without Christmas
I just don't want to know

THE WORKER

It's true to recall
whatever you do
there's always someone
that's worse off than you

It's hard to get work
when your only twelve
but if you tell lies
your age you can shelve

When dad passed away
mum and sis alone
just one pound fifty
the income for home

Took me a long time
and many a frown
to turn Liverpool
almost upside down

Yet it's strange to say
got a starting date
with Russian tailor
next Monday at eight

So twelve and sixpence
my wages for a week
both mum and Liz pleased
Give them both a treats

When Harry Brassey
then gave me the nod
it's hooray at last
finally got job

TOO SHORT 1949

National Service
done it at last
but got no job
it's in the past

So into town
and see what's there
as I need work
just anywhere

Outside Cop Shop
could this be me
courage I need
go in and see

Then tell the boss
what looking for
he shakes his head
says stand by door

I follow orders
and stand by door
boss shakes his head
says need six more

It seems six foot
a coppers height
six inches short
I shrink from sight

GHOST OF CHRISTMAS PAST

Will the ghost
of Christmas past
haunt me to
the very last
I was young
and times were hard
Christmas feared
so little shared
just our luck
and with it stuck
shop windows
they were a treat
full of things
we'd never meet
will the ghost
of Christmas past
recall kids
that he walked past

THE DREAMER

They called me a dreamer
I suppose that is right
as I've always wanted
just everything in sight

As a boy shop windows
all chock a block with toys
wide eyes take it all in
and lots of stuff for boys

Even more at Christmas
the windows full to brim
gang of kids around them
like me just looking in

Even kids understand
that what they see not yours
but memory holds the key
to unlock day dream doors

TOUGH IN THE PAST

Born in the past
that twenty nine
and hard times too
poverty time

My early life
in Liverpool
two sis and me
we go to school

Dad a soldier
crippled in war
tiny pension
was all he saw

Me almost ten
and still can't read
but world war two
has been conceived

WHERE

Can't find the answer
and looked very hard
it may surprise you
in your back yard

And always reasons
for things that we do
always an answer
that may escape you

OUR CHRISTMAS

It's Christmas on the street
not the best place to be
but life can put you there
it could be you or me

Sometimes it is money
could be you don't fit in
the family discard you
and put you in the bin

Lots of us sleeping rough
there's men and women too
cuddled up in doorways
how we'll see Christmas through

We've ex-service men too
who can't quite settle down
parted from their families
who live in far off town

Many welfare helpers
who give us food and cash
soup kitchens a God send
we'll survive winters blast

It gets dark traffic gone
it's time to dream of home
but we know cannot go
tomorrow still alone

It's Christmas on the street
should not be here at all
we don't know the answer
ask God to bless us all

LIVERPOOL

Liverpool
where I was born
a northern town
which many scorn

Has buildings new
and buildings old
but people's hearts
are solid gold

It started round
about King John
alas the castles
have all gone

Slavers sailed
in days of old
a human cargo
in the hold

And sold them far
across the sea
a busy trade
in misery

Now all this
is in the past
good or bad times
never last

Well known people
by the score
have all gone through
this northern door

LIVERPOOL MEMORIES

Lots in the pool to see
some of it history

Two first teams a mile apart
cavern where Beatles start

Lots of shops to wander round
no cars in centre found

Lord Street got trees and seats
take your time enjoy treats

Art galleries to see
cafes there stop for tea

Museums St Georges Hall
down to pier head we call

Cruise liners waiting there
heading out who knows where

Ferry's on the Mersey too
see Liver Buildings view

Liver Birds watch Mersey
on its way to the sea

LIVERPOOL LIVERPOOL

Liverpool Liverpool
what have you done to me
sent me to the midlands
a long way from the sea

There's no Liver buildings
and there's no Mersey sound
St Georges hall missing
it's nowhere to be found

Liverpool Liverpool
what crime did I commit
born and bred a scouser
I thought I would fit

But the pools all go go
maybe I'm in the past
guess I'm getting tired
it's time for rest at last

FROM LIVERPOOL

From Liverpool
must be a fool
sense of humour
fantastic tool

You often hear
what people say
and many times
it make your day

Ask a copper
how long next bus
he'll look at watch
say thirty foot

Some folk serious
I know that true
can't be drinking
our local brew

I knew a girl
that liked to sing
and raise the roof
like anything

She went to sing
and sup at pub
after a few
she'd curse her hub

Alice the Malice
lost a good job
many joined her
have a good sob

THE SCOUSER'S PRAYER

Born in Liverpool
a long time ago
a sense of humour
a part of the show
life can be easy
life can be hard
the good times
and the bad times
you take by the yard
you can be happy
and give them a smile
people relax
it'll take you a mile
works hard to find
that's nothing new
your dad did the same
and stood in the queue
maybe you'll win it
maybe you won't
believe you can do it
and break all the rules
world's full of winners
and some of them fools
optimists always
we can't change our ways
a scouser forever
to the end of our days

LIVERPOOL SOUND

If I wander down
into my old town
will it be the same
the Liverpool sound
kind of gone to ground
Liver Birds don't fly
the proud streets I knew
where no flowers grew
gardens hard to find
homes two up two down
and close to the town
and two cathedrals
have hope street to share
and now the pool is
a teaching city
and students worldwide
will always have pride
taught in Liverpool

IS IT CHRISTMAS

It was Christmas
or so they say
just can't find it
it's lost its way

Hear bells ringing
and snow flakes fall
Christmas somewhere
I do recall

Carols ring out
across the snow
but where on earth
did Christmas go

LIZ AND I

So Liz and I
we must leave home
all kids must go
from danger zone

Everyone in street
by bus we go
Lime Street station
that place we know

As our teachers
load up the train
we all wonder
when back again

A MEMORY LANE

Follow me down
memory lane
see the good times
just once again

Had two sisters
I never see
far too busy
keep eye on me

Up and over
the back yard walls
and see some jam jars
my seat in stalls

Pocket money
none of us had
no one working
war injured dad

That Garden Street
in Liverpool
where poverty
appeared to rule

YESTERDAY 1936

Let us go back
to yesterday
in Liverpool
where we did stay

There times are hard
life could be tough
money you had
never enough

Whole neighbourhoods
struggled along
life on parish
it was no song

The years would come
and years would go
all will tell you
God doesn't know

Good shoes warm clothes
enough to eat
not permitted
down Garden Street

THIRTEEN SITE

A service camp in sixty one
with all its square cut lines
I will remember always
but not for drink or wines
but for the love that came to me
from one who really cared
who showed me deep sincerity
and how it should be shared
who took my hand and led me
through a strange and delicate world
where the spoken word is star dust
where the silver lining curled
and two blend gently into one
such happiness will soon be gone
come cast away conventions shrouds
to walk with me among the clouds
the jealous Gods forbid most mortals
to wander through their lofty portals

ABERFAN

On the twenty first it came
striking with the speed of flame
around the world was flashed the name
of death at Aberfan

The work and toil of many years
became a mountain rent with tears
confirming all the long felt fears
of death at Aberfan

Down it slithered crushing all
nothing stood before this wall
the school itself was seen to fall
such tears at Aberfan

And to the rescue thousands ran
to save the children as one man
the sweat and tears together ran
the streets of Aberfan

Some were saved but many died
God himself surely cried
to see the children trapped inside
the school of Aberfan

The noise has stopped and all is still
the children sleep upon the hill
where God can hold them closer till
they rebuild Aberfan

AT HOME 1936

Like many round here
a family we were
just like then others
we live on thin air

For those who could work
no work to be got
parish paid us
allowance we got

True we were grateful
for we would survive
many things missing
however you strive

Warm clothes and footwear
to see the winter through
a nice hot coal fire
these things not for you

As a seven year old
I was never told
of problems we had
each day it was sad

My dad could not work
injured in the war
still fighting for us
could not ask for more

CHRISTMAS COMES

Our Christmas comes
our Christmas goes
never the same
just full of woes

Some will like it
others will not
a special thought
Christmas has got

Carols and kids
and falling snow
nothing Like it
that I know

CHRISTMAS EVE

It's Christmas Eve
and silence reigns
frost all over
window frames

The world sleeps on
awaits the day
to celebrate
in every way

Father Christmas
a busy man
he does his best
for all he can

FOOTPRINTS IN THE SNOW

Say a prayer at Christmas
for those no longer here
only takes a minute
that surely you can spare

Could be friends or children
you've known a long long time
or part of the family
it could be yours or mine

So stop and think of them
no footprints in the snow
and only yours are there
as on your way you go

Say a prayer this Christmas
it will put you in touch
yesterday knows the way
memory loves so much

WEATHER UP N DOWN

Weather up
weather down
rain may tumble down
as we go to town
may be a change
from getting soaked

CHRISTMAS THOUGHTS 1936

Tis said the thought that counts
memory jarred perhaps
something you should have done
but buried in the past

Memories your diary
will tell you where and when
you'll remember most things
but slip up now and then

And take you to places
no longer there to see
where I lived as a boy
with all my family

Yet Dad and Mum still there
two sisters brother too
me six or seven then
and all this clear to you

This would be the thirties
and tough times to live through
Mum and Dad pure gold
so we all made it too

SHOPPING WITH MUM 1937

With mum to shop
it a rare thing
she wants bargains
on everything

She never bought
a pack of tea
dust from the bins
six pence would be

Expensive blends
all kinds of tea
so this the dust
six pence would be

Meat from the butcher
was far too dear
sixpence for bones
mum would prefer

Boil bones in pot
and veg too
next day dripping
as well for you

Cheap meat and fish
on Saturday get
when auctioned off
back of market

THE BACK STREETS 1936

The back streets of Liverpool
I would wander alone
there's lots of things to see
but unlikely to own

Paper shop my favourite
and toys there by the score
I just stand there dreaming
a shop what kids adore

Fish and chip shop next door
they wrap fish bits for me
even then smell lovely
for me and Liz free tea

So this was Paddington
ran next to Garden Street
and it climbed the hill
but at the top my thrill

New Palladium there
and if Liz take me in
see Shirley Temple there
who will make my heart spin

All the shops I need here
and home not far away
see Shirley now and then
now that would make my day

HOME IS WHERE YOU FIND IT

Home is where you find it
it may be far or near
not what you expected
the search can cost you dear

Quiet in Rhodesia
where crickets sing all night
busy town in England
its green fields sheer delight

Still I search through life's span
and will find it if I can
some fireside will welcome me
as only fireside can

THE DESERT STORY

Desert knows the story
and desert knows the song
wind whispers the secrets
he's known the desert long

Many different nations
have crossed it too and fro
many fierce battles
where fought out long ago

Hot by day cold by night
fantastic starlit sky
still leading the faithful
in all those years gone by

SOUTH AFRICA SUNSETS

And Africa
I do recall
the sunsets there
are free for all

Many colours
must be a score
sun goes down
can't count more

Cross the border
Rhodesia see
it's name has changed
to Zimbabwe

Kariba dam
will hold your breath
Victoria Falls
never forget

And Africa
was once my home
sunsets haunt me
when I'm alone

SALISBURY RHODESIA

Salisbury in summer
a most enchanting sight
the sidewalk cafes crowded
with people black and white

Yet war is round the corner
a contact in the bush
black and white are fighting
the terrorist to crush

The aged and the lonely
on isolated farms
are fair game for these people
who carry Russian arms

They massacre the natives
rob them left and right
incinerate their villages
and steal away at night

THE CHRISTMAS BEETLE-RHODESIA 1976

Settled in Rhodesia
and this a larger plot
round about five acres
so room we got a lot

Not seen any flowers
September planting time
summer here at Christmas
Opposite British time

Wanted sixty roses
to go along the front
took some time to get them
they say about a month

All hands there to plant them
down the front forty feet
pleased I'd got my roses
their scent would be a treat

Early in December
buds and flowers in bloom
not believe disaster
would strike my plants so soon

That night swarms of beetles
just like the English bee
descended on roses
and left just storks for me

RHODESIA 1976 CONVOYS

Rhodesia unsettled
but talking not at war
Government trying hard
and some folk wanted more

Two tribes seeking power
to pull country apart
both supplied with weapons
from overseas at start

Some troubles in the bush
and isolated farms
all ready for trouble
whenever there's alarms

Some large towns surrounded
the roads blocked in and out
our troops search all traffic
for weapons they look out

All transport to and fro
line up at eight and go
guarded by the army
their weapons all on show

Troops with all the convoys
and traffic town to town
we all travelled safely
our lads don't let us down

HOME IN AFRICA

Could be country
and could be town
must be somewhere
to settle down

Home Africa
Rhodesia too
lovely weather
but home not true

Has great sunsets
colour's galore
an old cottage
that I'd adore

THE DESERT

It was long long ago
and whispered by the wind
secrets of the deserts
where many many sinned

Armies by the thousand
had battled for the land
and many found their graves
were scattered in the sand

Wind says it never change
that man shall battle man
desert very quiet
wind see no sign of man

THE WIND

Wind can blow the sand
alter all the dunes
whisper in your ear
long forgotten tunes

War in the desert
pharaohs and their queens
pyramids on show
such different scenes

Fantastic buildings
wind has seen before
one day will blow away
and be seen no more

Wind knows the silk road
those who travel far
and recalls three kings
searching for a star

Wind knows Africa
and it's wealth galore
where gold and diamonds
lay along its shore

The skeleton coast
well known for its wrecks
the sea very fierce
not what ships expect

Wind is so tired
goes down with the sun
as it also sets
in a golden west

AFRICA

Africa is silent
sleeping in the sun
yet many strangers come
and many have a gun

Animals are slaughtered
many shores are dug for for gold
and diamonds can be found
just scattered on the ground

Many people travel
these riches to secure
when they fear these stories
or riches on the floor

Africa is doubtful
these people come and go
take away my riches
Africa they don't know

Sunrise in the mourning
fantastic coloured sky
starlight in the evening
sunset bids goodbye

AFRICA AFRICA

Africa Africa
oh why do you haunt me
your sea shores and deserts
full of diamonds and gold

Your richer than many
your history so old
and many the secrets
the wind has never told

It's witch doctors are there
and still throwing the bones
to tell you the future
in many grass built homes

Africa Africa
you will sleep in the sun
a proud land for many
under Africa's sun

RHODESIA 1975

Rhodesia asleep
quiet in the sun
war around the corner
we all have a gun

It's independence
African intend Ian Smith Rule
Smith rules quite stable
Britain not content

Two tribes are fighting
each other to rule
China and Russia
supply the weapons pool

Seems they are ready
face us with a gun
Britain still thinking
Smith says carry on

Whole country backs him
well liked everywhere
Rhodesia is British
we'll all do our share

IN THE AFRICAN HEART

Africa Africa
on a warm starlit night
the crickets are chirping
but nowhere in sight
the moon has spread silver
on rivers far below
but what are you thinking
tell me what do you know
strangers came ploughed the land
that was good that was grand
yet others dig the ground
till precious stones are found
others seek yellow gold
then I see war has come
farmers just need a gun
crops are not gathered in
end of war no one win
all are free peace at last
now thousands heading west
they say life there is best
wish them well time will tell
but they'll remember me

IN AFRICA I DREAM

The spirit of Africa
standing in the rain
contemplating freedom
contemplating pain

The spirit of Africa
whither shall you go
along the path the spirit points
only you can know

The spirit of Africa
inscrutable to the last
pondering the future
pondering the past

The spirit of Africa
quiet and serene
I wonder what you're thinking
I wonder what you dream

R L I RHODESIAN LIGHT INFANTRY

Up on the border
and down the dusty roads
In jungle greens they can be seen
fighting dusky foes

Early in the morning
and sometimes late at night
tackling the terrorist
whenever he's in sight

No room for the squeamish
nor room for the rules
a bullet cannot recognize
the brainy from the fools

It's simply kill or be killed
and who can argue there?
there's no such thing as heroes
you're petrified with fear

ISCOR STEEL (SOUTH AFRICA)

The stars grow dim and dawn is nigh
chimneys belching smoke on high
seem to whisper and to sigh
under an Iscor sky

Buses threading to and fro
a shift to come a shift to go
many grateful for a blow
under an Iscor sky

Faces black and faces white
producing steel with all their might
this a multiracial sight
under an Iscor Sky

Many nations share this toil
of making plate, bar and coil
united on a foreign soil
under an Iscor Sky

THE GREEN FIELDS OF ENGLAND

The green fields of England
I remember to this day
so long since I saw them
the years have flown away

There's beauty in the tropics
and many sights to see
but the green fields of England
my heart can ache for thee

I've seen the Zulu warriors
pulling rickshaw chairs
and down by Durban harbour
the natives sell their wares

The southern cross can sparkle
like jewels in the sky
but the green fields of England
are the apple of my eye

JOHANNESBURG

Johannesburg the golden city
sparkling in the sun
a mixture of all the races
and a haven for the gun

The centre of South Africa
a complex business world
on the pavement fast asleep
a beggar's child is curled

Busy mines producing gold
their waste dumps rearing high
digging deep inside the reef
a thirst to satisfy

Johannesburg the golden city
as twilight turns to night
sparkling with a million neons
deserted till daylight

TO GROW A LIFE

To grow a life
difficult thing
to catch a bird
that's on the wing

But bring a child
into the world
always there
as life unfurls

And dad by day
you show the way
avoid the path
where problems lay

Wont be easy
and can be hard
to grow a life
in your backyard

But it is yours
always will be
and they call it
responsibility

I WANDER THROUGH

I wander through
the world alone
still not find
that place called home

In busy towns
country places
there is no sign
or even traces

In foreign parts
like Africa
I've spent some time
but still no sign

Could be missed it
a busy day
always at work
and need the play

I don't give up
it must be found
then home at last
well I'll be bound

But not there yet
so I plod on
into the future
my search goes on

A HOME

It's just a dream
when I'm alone
thinking of a
place that was home

England and Wales
must of had two
South Africa
and Rhodesia too

A sunlit world
with lots to do
a lovely sunset
each night for you

Lots of places
to settle down
very far from
my own home town

But time goes bye
the years roll on
and Africa
my number one

A PAGE

Paper paper
talk to me
you've been around
crossed the sea
left the forest
as a tree
don't see sunshine
any more
or hear the rain
when it pour
the sky has gone
no moon see
I was happy
as a tree
to find me look
in any book
a page can't cry
it's goodbye
enjoy your book

RHODESIA

A diamond in the sun
your world was torn apart
and war for everyone
some lived and many died
Cecil Rhodes surely cried
to see his world on fire
Africa took it's gem
Rhodesia is long gone
the wind whispers farewell
a diamond in the sun
has set for every one

A BOOK

A book can be your world
take you across the seas
and visit strange places
go anywhere you please

Have a look at Egypt
and pyramids you'll see
then China has a wall
a visitor you'll be

Africa lots to see
Victoria falls don't miss
skeleton coast must see
always in memory

Easter Island statues
they stare across the sea
to pay them a visit
to find out what they see

But don't miss Yellowstone Park
deep canyons water worn
old volcano still lives
and lots of steam still born

A POEM

To hold a poem
in your hand
you'll find it easy
to understand
it can tell you a story
from beginning
to end
it can be a stranger
it can be a friend
It can show you
our world
in so many ways
a multitude of people
different every one
all part and parcel
of our race
it's called
the human one

TRUE

So don't lose sight
of what is right
always be fair
don't tear your hair

Mistakes you'll make
as most folks do
but you be you
whatever you do

ALONE

I've wandered far
and search alone
and cannot find
what I'd call home

I've loved and lost
can't count the cost
I just don't know
why this is so

I've given all
but always fall
when eyes of blue
say I love you

But then one day
you'll hear her say
I can't be true
I don't love you

I stumble on
and can't find one
to make a home
I'm still alone

SMITH CORONA

Smith Corona
why do you roam
surely happy
with Yvonne at home

Said like to work
with lots to do
I'm not retired
so looked for you

Your just the job
a poets dream
happy typing
ream after ream

And no mistake
we are a team
Smith Corona
a poets dream

THE TROUBADOUR

Story tellers
some years ago
found life easy
so had a go

Lots of people
would gather round
in the pub
or on the ground

But some would gasp
the things he said
about people
alive or dead

Sometimes an hour
or two went by
and now and then
a girl would cry

It took a while
to tell a tale
as pennies fall
into his pail

Always welcome
this troubadour
he has stories
by the score

MEMORY LANE

A well known name
but just a game
played by us all

We loved the past
that cannot last
but we recall

The times we shared
with those that cared
but cannot call

But down the lane
they still the same
welcome a call

WOULD NOT GO

There was a man
would would not die
a pain to all
who made Fate cry

He never where
that he should be
then fate gave up
and set him free

Twas heard he said
too much for me
far too busy
white hair I'll be

THE PEN

Pen has all the answers
and all the reasons why
I can only guide it
with a tear in my eye

Many words are written
and some are sad to see
tragedy and heartache
not good for you or me

Pen must tell the story
of love beyond recall
if life or death involved
then loved ones must know all

And pen is the agent
for it will bring the news
of world wide disasters
to papers that you choose

Pen can be personal
the tragedy your own
as you write through the tears
just want to be alone

A STORY

Life is a story
a page every day
some pages busy
some with time to play

Pages for summer
some for winter too
some cover Christmas
and New Year for you

A day at a time
should work out just fine
you may miss a day
if you like your wine

If this is the case
you are in disgrace
your pages galore
all on bar-room floor

THE POEM IN ME

The poem wants to have a home
for many years it's been alone
and wandered round for countless years
now and then it's seen the tears
readers come and readers go
very few will say hello
or ask me where I'd like to be
it could be you, it could be me
I could make you laugh as you read away
and cheer you up on a rainy day
cuddle up on a winter's night
when all outside is pristine white
and never ever go away
just looking for a shelf to stay

DON'T LOOK BACK

Don't look back
nothing there
good times gone
bad times stare
you make it
or you wont
win it
or you don't
it's today
not yesterday
can't live there
face your world
have no fear

RIDE THE WIND

Ride the wind
and travel far
doesn't matter
who you are
spin around
the world
in style
see the Congo
and the Nile
scorching deserts
far below
rain-soaked forests
an Amazon show
east wind wants
to show the way
see the icebergs
on display
polar bears
and arctic hares
this land of ice and snow
is theirs
we spin around
and heading east
incredible journey
a traveller's feast

DEBRIS

Look beyond the city limits
leave the busy streets behind
there you'll find the blasted rubble
forgotten years it brings to mind

Even those who can remember
rarely pass this way again
for the sound of screaming sirens
still echo in this broken lane

And the shells of gutted buildings
stark and clear against the sky
bear silent witness to destruction
their war torn shoulders cannot lie

WORLD WAR ONE

It was a war to end wars
on everybody's lips
but many many slips
just death and destruction
morning noon and night
thousands blown to pieces
to stay alive you fight
you live in the trenches
the cold and mud are there
tomorrow is not ours
for then we face the storm
waiting for the whistle
a front line trench at dawn

1918

Some will go to the front
some will know they'll fall
no other way to answer
when duty makes that call

All belong to someone
with families at home
and hard to forget them
deep in this battle zone

Sarge says get your heads down
this quiet cannot last
jerry's planning something
make sure you check your mask

Hear the sound of music
mouth organ players fine
soon we all start singing
it's Tipperary time

Sun goes down fags light up
we all have thoughts of home
what will tomorrow bring
will loved ones be alone

Four am check our gear
well aware jerry's near
ladders against our wall
waiting for whistle call

Whistle blew at half past four
we are up and over
and as machine guns crossfire
you've got to hit the floor

Our shells now just ahead
you lay flat or your dead
the shells whine and scream past
at enemy ahead

So our guns on the job
have given them a smack
a new dawn is breaking
wont bring our comrades back

THE CIRCLE

Gone are the good times
and I don't know where
here are the bad times
and there everywhere

But life is not meant
to have fun and games
it doesn't matter
if folk call you names

Have a good reason
to do what you do
and let them down
who depend on you

We all have duty
and must see it through
and never forgotten
they rely on you

Life is a circle
your children are there
and when you grow old
they'll recall your care

WORLD WAR ONE - GONE

The mist is still there
and the poppies too
the trenches silent
where the whistle blew

And many are those
who have lost their lives
always expected
with every sunrise

Families in mourning
for those not come back
hard times much harder
a father they lack

A soldier gives all
whatever the task
he'll run through the mist
it may be his last

The mist is still there
empty trenches too
can we ever learn
to reject war too

A LIFE IN WAR

A life for a life
or what is war for
to kill or be killed
that evens the score

And no one wants it
every death counts
life is forgotten
when enemy pounce

Women and children
don't matter at all
if you are at war
death will take them all

Some nations warlike
optimists must be
each soldier's badge says
that god is with me

ALWAYS WAR

War not good at all
many people fall
death and destruction
to answer the call

Sometimes religion
or use of the sword
bring us to our knees
war none can afford

Simple rules to follow
death to you or me
soldier don't argue
or he's history

War not a new thing
very very old
hard to love neighbour
wants you dead and cold

Seems our human race
one day face to face
learn love our neighbour
or end of human race

A SOLDIER'S WALK

I walk
no one behind me
I walk
with no one in front
I trust
only my shadow
I trust
my courage is there
I'll lead
into the battle
I'll bleed
like all of you will
I fear
death all around us
I too
may fall to the ground
I too
salute the soldier
for courage he found

IF THERE'S A BATTLE

If there's a battle
then it must be won
if your a soldier
you pick up your gun

No thoughts of your home
or family there
enemy's ready
and he is quite near

The whistle will blow
and up we will go
your seeking shelter
and face down you will go

Machine guns not stop
upright you'd be shot
the ground is wet mud
stay alive you should

Then the gunfire stops
and silence prevails
the morning mist
shows the brave who failed

WW1 LIVES

In a trench at dawn
1918 morn
it's cold and muddy
and sometimes bloody

No advance today
heavy shelling stay
cup of tea and fag
then the time wont drag

Sometimes sing a song
wonder just how long
this war can go on
neither side has won

Many lives are lost
such a tragic cost
welcome morning sun
one more day we've won

RETURN

Return to sender
address unknown
I've searched for years
but can't find home

THE SEA

The sea a massive grave
with World War One and Two
earthquakes and eruptions
increase the death rate too

Ships submarines and more
never got back to shore
these brave souls by the score
never expected more

Millions served millions died
countless the eyes that cried
for those not make it home
under the sea alone

A SOLDIER

If your a soldier
you can do no more
than fight to the death
on a foreign shore

It's sometimes easy
and tough luck if hard
seconds can save you
must be on your guard

The enemy is there
and not far away
may have to meet him
down our street one day

OUR WORLD

The world is ours
but temperatures rise
should we ignore this
that would not be wise

Weather is changing
and the floods worldwide
the major countries
just cannot decide

Our ways must alter
or our world is gone
and is heading for
our last setting sun

AUTUMN ARRIVES

When autumn comes
the trees have fear
they know winter
is very near

A gentle wind
blows golden leaves
and scatters them
beneath the trees

Goodbye summer
you've had your day
wind says winter
is on it's way

PLASTIC A PROBLEM

Plastic bags can travel
and nowhere they can't go
around the world and back
the best routes they will know

But birds are suffering
and fish are caught up too
these years of plastic
some thing we will rue

Mariana trench deep
around six miles or more
yet plastic waste found there
just lying on the floor

Plastic is a problem
we all use far too much
maybe brown paper bags
are what we need so much

WINTER WHISPER

Wind will whisper
among the trees
and knows the news
it will not please

The leaves have gone
all blown away
but the winter
is on its way

The falling snow
will blanket all
for miles around
with just one fall

All is quiet
the trees will sleep
till spring returns
its promise keep

CLIMATE DANCE

Summer winter
go hand in hand
one day is cold
the next day is grand

Worldwide friendship
that is a fact
when together
our climate whacked

What's the answer
where you might go
summer winter
dance to and fro

Chaos worldwide
and no mistake
fires and floods
stay in their wake

WEATHER WEATHER

Weather weather
it's cold or hot
can't make its mind up
what have we got

Your not the same
a trusted friend
and drive us all
around the bend

You say our fault
what can we do
must change our ways
and worldwide too

Take a long time
to get it right
a labour of love
well worth the fight

ALWAYS TOMORROW

Put it off
till tomorrow
tis said it never comes
that suit us fine
we'll have
a lot more time
pay that bill of mine

CLIMATE

The world spins on
but does it care
lots of people
will foul its air

They're burning oil
and coal and gas
it lift the temp
of climate fast

Forest fires
are quite severe
thousands of trees
a loss we fear

There's floods and storms
we're not used to
world together
we might pull through

Will take some years
to get it right
then climate change
put out of sight

CLIMATE CHANGE

Summers gone but where
climate change is here
yet some let it grow
world knows it is so

It has been severe
quite dangerous too
all pull together
we can change weather

And there seems no doubt
earth hard to replace
balance of nature
lost by human race

OUR WEATHER

Life keeps on changing
nothing stays the same
maybe all end up
lost down memory lane

Whole world affected
climate up and down
floods and fires frequent
some islands drown

All know the answer
entire world take part
change way of living
make a brilliant start

WEATHER

Weather weather
get together
just one or two
that will not do

It's bad world wide
the sun may hide
and floods galore
with lots lots more

We need an ear
to bellow down
get this sorted
before we drown

TOMORROW

If you find tomorrow
the kindly let me know
for I lost it somewhere
it took time off to go

I had things to sort out
and the problem quite clear
look around its missing
tomorrows disappeared

Have to get another
and pin it to the wall
can't have them skipping off
not good enough at all

CLIMATE JOURNEY

Every journey
will have an end
every cloud
the rain will send

But things change
nature not cope
fumes we produce
will make earth choke

Trees that's needed
are burnt down too
Amazon fires
what can we do

Unite the world
to change their ways
if it doesn't
earth ends its days

MANY WAYS TO TRAVEL

Many ways to travel
and may be just to work
another day to fill
a way to pay the bill

EARTH FUTURE

All expect a future
for many there is none
as ageing and illness
will take it's toll of some

Few of us are ready
to say the last goodbye
many things need to do
and many asking why

Body takes wear and tear
through the years some repair
life can be extended
but its time to take care

Go out enjoy your world
and if life short or long
it's a place of beauty
this earth where you belong

WARMING WEATHER

Islands are at risk
some will disappear
weather earth warming
it's a double risk
but quick action soon
will stop earth slipping
to a future doom

EARTH LONG AGO

Long long ago
when earth was young
no life was here
and no bird sung

The sun by day
the moon by night
they watched the earth
with great delight

Animals fish
and great birds too
covered the earth
some fierce true

The dinosaurs
where everywhere
all animals
would live in fear

Alas one day
meteor struck
enormous size
the whole earth shook

And darkness came
no sunlight shone
the end for some
dinosaurs gone

SEPTEMBER

September in the rain
I know you'll come again
and remember

The day we both would get
completely soaking wet
never forget

So hurry back to me
the raindrops I can see
welcoming me

September and you there
blue eyes and golden hair
we're together

SEPTEMBER SO TENDER

Nothing so tender
and nothing more true
than that September
that I spent with you

Always together
we walk through the rain
with anyone else
would not be the same

Gold hair sparkles
with last rays of sun
and blue eyes tell me
that I am the one

OUR EARTH

Earth a solo planet
travels through space each day
moon her only companion
and never far away

Our earth knows the heavens
and travels well known track
will follow her orbit
and no time to look back

Often facing danger
but cannot step aside
meets the problem head on
then brushes it aside

Her journey to the sun
a challenge to be won
earth a long time in space
her orbit to the sun

ANIMALS

Some folks
scared of
animals
whose eyes
can magnify
and make a bigger you

COLLISION 10,950BC

It's carved in stone
for all to see
massive comet
makes history

Woolly mammoths
they have all gone
Earth in the dark
where is the sun

A new ice age
has just begun
our frozen world
heads for the sun

Stars and comets
chiselled out too
southern Turkey
know this is true

THE FUTURE

Look into
the future
a dodgy thing
to do
what's hiding there
could be a blow
you don't want to know

OUR CLIMATE

Sun is missing
often not here
winter long gone
summer is where

Some countries flooded
yet others stone dry
havoc created
and climate change why

A massive problem
can world change its ways
because if not
its the end of our days

THE SPINNING WORLD

The world spins on it's way
quite nonchalant I'd say
a date and time to keep
that's heading for the sun

It's peoples come and go
ice ages come also
frozen earth not deterred
it's journey must go on

Many times battered
collapsing stars shatter
earth will journey on
destiny the sun

INDEPENDENT WEATHER

Weathers independent
it don't like you or me
wind will blow us off course
and soaked we all will be

A day may be sunny
you trot out for a walk
then rain hail and thunder
you can't hear yourself talk

Weather takes the mickey
has loads and loads of fun
nice day can go astray
and rain soak every one

WINTER

It seems the nights are drawing in
the evening air a trifle thin
summer has given of her best
winter awaits her last request
autumn holds the keys

All the beauty warmth and sunlight
scented roses in the twilight
all things growing in confusion
face at last the same conclusion
winters mysteries

THE ICE AGE

Into the glass the young man stared
and saw the world grow old
before his very eyes the sun
had suddenly grown cold

A darkness greater than the night
plunged everything into gloom
and bitter cold came creeping in
the once familiar room

He looked again and dimly saw
the ocean's crumbled bed
littered with a million wrecks
on which the urchins fed

Become a snow-white blanket now
as flakes began to fall
they settled on the broken earth
a shroud to cover all

Through the mist of frozen white
the young man saw no sign
of living creatures on earth
there was no trace or kind

The grip of ice had strangled
all that lived and grew
and brought the silence of the grave
to a world that never knew

The young man slowly turned away
so troubled was his soul
as he beheld an ice-cold world
begin to spin and roll

Free of its orbit chains at last
it sped into the night
onto its own destruction
a brilliant flash of light

THE EARTH

The earth was battered
day and night
yet no enemy
was in sight
continuous sunspots
was the cause
and made the
earth almost pause
plant growth nearly
on the verge
and farming crops
a sudden surge
nature's balance
off the scales
the life of fish
endangered too
people don't know
what to do
as temperature falls
day by day
then all the world for
rain will pray
all ships in port
and no planes fly

we've never known
an empty sky
it's summer now
the ice still there
soon we'll have
the winter here
to survive we
all must go
into the caves
and far below
the surface is
no place to be
food and water
we stock plenty
many things we
must put by
till we see
a clear blue sky
our icy world
speeds on its way
towards the sun
so far away

EARTH

Have you got time
to stand a while
and watch the world
spin by
observe it at a distance
perhaps you'd wonder why
it has its hot
and cold days
a climate wet and dry
seas that team with many fish
and forests by the score
mountains reaching to the sky
snow capped and very high
a multitude of people
a variety of life
a small and lonely world
we speed through
time and space
the mother of
the human race
earth

PROBLEM

If you have a problem
and cannot sort it out
lets be fair find a chair
good kip you need no doubt

ROSES IN THE RAIN

In a garden far away
where we used to sit and play
I wonder if we'll ever be the same
how I held you close and cared
and we talked of things we shared
and you showed me the roses in the rain
there was beauty there was grace
there was magic in this place
and I knew my life would never be the same
till we are once again at play
in that garden far away
and together see the roses in the rain

RAIN

As I looked up the clouds came by
scudding through a rainswept sky
a host of tears it seemed to cry
a melancholy thought
the smallest brook will rumble loud
resembling an angry crowd

Its swollen waters very proud
too busy to cavort
now a shaft of brilliant light
has put the rainclouds into flight
the sun's sparkling world will sight
a rainbow it has caught

AUTUMN

From these heights it seems a crown
of russet gold green and brown
has settled on the hills

All around the trees have fear
they surely know that winter's here
and prepare for its chills

The wind so gently stirs the leaves
their carpet thick beneath the trees
seemingly forlorn

Of all the seasons to compare
only autumn gold can share
blunting winter's dawn

NEVER

Never mind the weather
and never mind the rain
we will stay together
the sun will shine again
we'll live life on the run
and chase the clouds away
now that's a holiday

THE WIND IS A FRIEND

The wind is a friend
saw the beginning
and observe the end

Wind saw many wars
and not understand
what could be the cause

Knows the deep seas
and tiny islands
gives palm trees a breeze

As the sun goes down
in a golden west
tired wind also rests

THE PERFECT YOU

And confidence
is all you need
to surge ahead
and take the lead
and what you do
just do it right
never argue
or pick a fight
you'll find that you
have got it right

SOMEONE

When fates been unkind
and things on your mind
it's never too late to recall
there's someone who dares
to shoulder your cares
when you find your backs to the wall

You can't journey on
and last hope has gone
just lift up your eyes to the sky
someone will be there
with welcoming tear
and waiting till he heard you cry

So just try and smile
you'll find in a while
the while world is smiling with you
someone to be sure
has opened the door
of happiness specially for you

BEAUTY

Beauty not forever
can steal away one night
and disappear at dawn
leaving you forlorn

CLIMATE NEEDS

Take the time to wonder
what we are heading to
lock downs and virus
the odd flood or two

Virus world problem
and climate change more
all have to unite
or world be no more

Vaccine the answer
it can lead the way
nations together
help our climate stay

DREAMS

Dreams what you make them
may never come true
all of us do it
when we feel blue

Dreams can be mobile
or go on a train
to that special place
memory lane

You roll back the time
and look through the tears
my one and only
lover appears

DREAM VALLEY

We all can go there
Its not far away
get rid of problems
just throw them away

Away from the world
or that's how it seems
everyone calls it
the valley of dreams

You can take your pick
have long or short stay
you can dream all night
you can dream all day

So grab your pillow
and be off to bed
you'll find dream valley
almost straight ahead

GOODBYE

It's hard to say goodbye
to someone you know well
as death could be quite near
so how are you to tell

Life just going steady
then suddenly full stop
not what you expected
it can be quite a shock

Someone you could chat to
and known a long long time
member of family
it could be yours or mine

Wont see them tomorrow
and made their last trip home
nothing left but sorrow
and we are more alone

GONE

The clock ticks bye
and time rolls on
should not waste it
once gone its gone

Was I success
a doubtful start
had no schooling
sets you apart

But lots of ways
to win the day
and make little
of needed pay

But times will change
and your alone
will need to move
another home

It's hard to do
and ageing too
end of a world
and that is true

Still time goes by
I give a sigh
life's a puzzle
and wonder why

NIGHT ON THE STREET

As night comes down
and darkness falls
streets are quiet
a car horn calls

People are few
we wont be seen
in a doorway
a sleepers dream

Lots of sleepers
are on the streets
just cant manage
so its defeat

Some will help us
bring food around
from passers by
get the odd pound

I huddle close
against my door
hope it won't rain
hope it won't pour

And it's midnight
might get some sleep
the world goes by
those on the street

OUTSIDE

Sleeping on the streets not good
no one in their right mind would
can't dodge the rain or the storm
that's only place to go

Seems no one wants to know
some folks fussy who' they touch
wear what we can don't have much
summer OK winter tough

Shop doorways are good enough
and when you leave tidy up
so next time you pass us by
remember it could be I

FORGET

If things don't go your way
maybe a storm ahead
you can do what I do
step off the world instead

Seek a different sunrise
another moon and sky
it's your favourite planet
well I can dream cant I

Stars sparkle above
and brilliant worlds near by
your problems forgotten
I can dream can't I

THE STREETS

The streets of London
are not paved with gold
and poverty there
you'll find taking hold
many use the street
a doorway will do
it's somewhere to sleep
little protection too
from wind rain and snow
the old and the young
who fell through life's net
they don't expect help
and little they get
government may know
and maybe they care
many citizens
poverty to share

A PRAYER

Many people
will say a prayer
to find answer
when in despair
when things go wrong
they ask for help
and raise their eyes
up to the skies
faith will tell them
if yes or no
was prayer answered
but they will know

IF A WISH

If you could have
a wish come true
what would it be
that would suit you

Is health and wealth
the number one
not getting old
that should be fun

Around the world
I'd like to sail
climb a mountain
no that I'd fail

And run around
in Timbuktu
shout at locals
how do you do

Can see my friends
deserting me
rich and nutty
I seem to be

EYES

Eyes tell a story
but only for you
guide you through your world
tell you what to do

Safely through traffic
driving or on foot
watching the lights change
seeking a short cut

Eyes can send message
look you up and down
if they don't like you
every chance they'll frown

But if they love you
you'll know that they care
show admiration
with you every where

A THOUGHT

Sometimes a thought
can save a tear
if it can reach
that saddened ear
of those who lost
a lifelong friend
trying to contemplate
the end

FOREVER

Said he'd live forever
but difficult to know
because he was certain
like us he would not go

Many asked him questions
how could he be so sure
he'd smile change the subject
he'd heard that one before

Others thought his secret
was just the job for them
but he'd not divulge it
some disappointed men

He lived near the sea
and often walked the shore
then one day he vanished
and was seen no more

Body not recovered
his secret was also gone
sea could know the answer
may know but tell no one

NO TIME

And time is something
never seem to have
comes goes quietly
be it good or bad

Memory recalls
the good times we had
won't dwell on bad times
if they very sad

Life like a fairground
many ups and downs
wend our way through it
knowledge will be found

STARS

There's a blanket
of stars in sight
that tuck me
and say good night

And I wonder
how far they are
tiny twinkle
from distant star

Will we ever
go there and see
what mystery
twinkle can be

A DREAM LONG AGO

So long ago
and far away
I dreamed a dream
that flew away

And no matter
whatever tried
could not catch it
before it died

And strange to say
I knew that face
the golden hair
the gentle grace

Flashed through my life
so long ago
those big blue eyes
that first hello

Then the storm clouds
they built up fast
impossible
our love to last

Maybe one day
we'll meet again
just you and me
memory lane

DUTY

So go your way
and don't look back
futures distant
no time to slack

A busy life
will see you through
little time for
those day dreams too

Family to feed
and bills to pay
sometimes wonder
can lose my way

I make ends meet
and that's a feat
have Sundays off
and that's my treat

TO SAY GOODBYE

To say goodbye
is hard to do
someone you knew
who's life is through
on their last journey too

FORGET ME

Forget Me
I'll never forget you
dreams we had together
It's sad they wont come true

We both climbed a rainbow
and had stars in our eyes
sure about the future
expecting no surprise

Said she'd go her own way
and different from mine
that I'd soon forget her
but will take a long time

PERFECTION

Some are borne lucky
follows them through life
win all kinds of things
pick a perfect wife

They don't make mistakes
always on the ball
loads and loads of friends
spirits never fall

They don't take chances
and bets always won
simply perfection
why can't I be one

CONTEMPLATION

Contemplation
can make you sad
thinking of what
you never had

And then again
I see a smile
I've beat others
by a good mile

Should be grateful
for what we've got
and not complain
if not a lot

So do cheer up
give it a guess
think fate has lost
your last address

So lucky you
there'll be some fun
just hit the road
and run run run

TIME GOES BY

And time goes by
boring to some
lifeline if many
find they've got none

We all get there
and no return
ways of the world
not our concern

Our memory
that stored for years
good and bad times
and lots of tears

Will close book
and heave a sigh
and give the world
our last goodbye

HOME TO SETTLE DOWN

Lots of places
to settle down
could be country
could be town
or far away
on palm fringed isle
that surely is my style

JUST A NURSE

If you see a flash of blue
going through the wards at two
go back to sleep
it's nothing new
just a nurse

If you're desperate for a crutch
and the pain has got too much
there's someone with a gentle touch
just a nurse

I only hope that when I die
and head towards that clear blue sky
I'll have an angel real close by
Just a nurse

NHS

You care for us
from cradle to grave
and many times
its lives that you save
not too busy
be it day or night
to hold a hand
or whisper good night
you walk the wards
from dusk into dawn
nurse is not made
a nurse must be born

A MOTHER

A mother's love is something pure
not easy to describe
for she'll go through fire and water
if her children so decide
no matter what they do or say
she'll never let them down
no matter how they treat her
on them she'll rarely frown
her love's past understanding
except perhaps to her
for only she will really know
of the pain she had to bear

MUMS

Girls never hide beauty
it's more precious than gold
with you such a short time
and gone when you grow old

Guard a generation
by leading them through life
avoiding the problems
and avoiding the strife

Their reward is children
to populate the earth
none do a better job
we all know what mums worth

CORONA VIRUS

All is quiet
and all is still
the empty streets
have time to kill

Where's the people
and traffic too
It's the virus
they will tell you

Crowds are not good
and sports cut out
keep folk apart
what it's about

Isolation
may stop the spread
whole world fights it
but thousands dead

Bug and climate
our world must fight
God help us all
to get it right

SLEEPING GIANTS

The giants asleep
on the ocean bed
and when they wake up
many may be dead

Massive volcanoes
that grumble and groan
are on the sea floor
where they made their home

New Zealand at risk
and Tokyo too
both places are watched
if eruption due

Wellington at risk
thousands need to know
and millions also
if Tokyo blow

A HOLIDAY

A holiday
have some fun in
and some out
far off place I'll stay
lots of sea
and lots of sand
ice cream
and palm trees
I'll understand
do I hear
a steel drum band

SOMETIMES TIMES

I sometimes think
that time stands still
and as a boy
I have no will
to join others
who in their teens
just have no time
for childish scenes
but I'm happy
when here or home
alas always
just on my own

TEA CLIPPER

Ships of the past
a tale to tell
as through the storm
they battle well
all heard lookout
as he did yell
see rocks ahead
give wheel a spin
the ship spun round
and the tea safe
in gale force wind
the captain grinned

OLD CAT

Good times
they come
and they go
and cost money
it can be a blow
sometimes the cash
for this
and for that
we can forget
look after the cat
always remember that
our old faithful cat

ZIMBABWE

Zimbabwe
sleeping
in the sun
to Cecil Rhodes
it was home
his dream
but lost
to everyone
at last it
had to end
the people pride
could not defend

RHODESIAN MINERALS

Gold and diamonds
to be found
and sapphires
on the ground
and in
the rivers
many fish
to be found

GETTING OLD

Money I need
what have I got
to be honest
not a lot
its a shame
a holiday
would cheer me up
in every way
got to save
for a long time
get enough
to pay for mine
and now at last
reach the day
mirror says
I'm old and grey

ZIMBABWE RELAX

A new name to Rhodesia
for Rhodesia
all settled at last
Africans
take over already
in the past
everyone nervous
how long will it last

THE COTTON MILLS

The cotton mills
of yesterday
their massive floors
are bare today
nobody work
there any more
came through that door
and ten year olds
were working too
helping parents
pay their way through
summer, winter
their work to do
a Blackpool hol
where all relax
a small reward
for breaking backs
it's only twice
the mills stand still
Christmas and hols
then all the mills will

THINK THE PAST

I think the past
best place to be
all you need
is memory
see those
you loved and lost
and things you did
with fingers crossed
see places known
no longer there
and meet that girl
with golden hair
all gone
but be seen
every time
I have a dream

VACCINE

Down the tunnel
the virus thrust
a beam of light
the vaccine pushed

A million sighs
the world has heaved
and God bless those
vaccine conceived

Difficult task
in record time
but saving lives
world wide is fine

PEOPLE

People loving people
wonderful world could be
holding hands together
what could be more friendly

All helping each other
world of comfort and care
all rewards divided
future all want to share

Many many nations
struggle their way through life
and happy to join us
and end the years of strife

All the world united
our flag is what we are
all the world salute it
a sparkling golden star

A TIME

A time to come
a time to go
a time for yes
a time for no
a time to laugh
a time to cry
be always right
some would you'd shun
no ones perfect
under the sun
meet some bright spark
every year
first of April
they will appear

THE DIVER

I knew a deep sea diver
who could no stand dry land
he said he liked it sloppy
with lots of fish around
not a lot of traffic
maybe a shark or two
they can be quite fussy
and never nibble you

JUST NITA

Just Nita
some folks stare
quiet voice
jet black hair

Just Nita
Irish too
her beauty
astound you

Just Nita
cares for son
if needed
on the run

Just Nita
full of fun
hair held high
in a bun

Just Nita
can surprise
such beauty
thoughtful eyes

Just Nita
Jack was two
her double
through and through

MY GUARDIAN ANGEL

I know its there
but don't turn round
know its there
for I heard a sound
it wont scare me
it can only be
my guardian angel

Things can go well
as they often do
and sometimes scary
but he sees me through
it don't worry me
it can only be
my guardian angel

Close calls I've had
on so many days
always been there
in a million ways
takes care of me
it can only be
my guardian angel

NITA

Nita lovely
and like a dream
most stunning girl
I've ever seen

Emerald eyes
and long black hair
she's a beauty
that make some stare

She holds the hand
of tiny son
who wondered why
that his dad has gone

Still together
Nita and son
into the future
a perfect mum

Publicity can be good
the Flying Scotsman said
while chatting with his pals
inside the engine shed

Can keep you on the rails
when belting down the track
that's why I got my name
I never never slack

I like a good head wind
and pressure more and more
top steam and a whistle
then Flying Scotsman score

THE FLYING SCOTSMAN

Flying Scotsman is the name
speeding on the rails his game
firebox glowing white hot now
racing over hill and brow
classic engine that's for sure
gives his best and maybe more
signals off as he goes past
bobbies know he's very fast
whistle blows he's off again
speeding north into the rain

TIME CAN BE A FRIEND

Time can be a friend
and enemy too
take your beauty
then you won't know you

We all face ageing
fight it every day
some folk don't bother
time will have his way

Yet we remember
beauty doesn't last
gone like yesterday
buried in the past

RIGHT GIRL

Sunlight tells a story
and moonlight tells a tail
both can be romantic
and never ever fail

But you need the right girl
to whisper in your ear
she will weather storms
and you will have no fear

She will give you comfort
on a cold wintry night
always there when needed
and never out of sight

RUFF AND TUFF

Ruff and tuff
a railway engine
to the core
he'll never tire
not many tracks
that he don't know
his whistle gets you
on the go
is very well known
on the rails
'tis said this
Scotsman never fails
snap your fingers
and he's gone
don't hang about
for anyone
speeding north
south, east or west
the bobbies think
he is the best
the whistle screams
and smoke galore
The Flying Scotsman
away once more

THE ENGINE FOR THE RAILS

Engine engine
talk to me
tell me where
and why you go
belching steam
and streaming smoke
awakening all
the country folk
your clicking wheels
can sing a song
no trip ever
very long
your whistle screams
as yet again
you're heading north
into the rain
other locos
on the rails
but the Flying Scotsman
never fails

THE ENGINE - 4472

Got to get there
he never fails
Flying Scotsman
racing the rails

Why the hurry
no other way
only so much
time in the day

Race through the night
hail rain or snow
he will get there
Scotsman can go

Loved by many
afraid of few
his whistle can
put wind up you

TIME WAITS

Time waits for no one
I tell you no lies
time has to answer
the fors and the whys

Love can enfold you
and carry you away
time cannot help you
if she will not stay

All your memories
and future as well
they can disappear
if time rings your bell

Time can be patient
it can understand
sometimes you'll need it
just times helping hand

THE STAR

I saw a star
on Christmas night
sparkling high
but just in sight

Sparkled for long
across the sky
towards the east
I don't know why

Was this the star
the three kings saw
leading them to
a stable door

It may be yes
it may be no
it was a long
long time ago

Alas my star
has gone from sight
it may return
next Christmas night

PERFECT

To be perfect
can be tricky
avoiding folk
who take micky

Must be clever
and very bright
always always
do get it right

And always smile
to say hello
may not know you
but you don't know

To be perfect
can be a strain
and guaranteed
to give you pain

SPOOKS

It's said that spooks
can give you fright
they are around
at darkest night

Haunted houses
will tell you more
you need to step
inside the door

It's said that they
can walk through walls
and float around
some ancient halls

If I met one
it's hard to tell
just see me run
extremely well

WORK

To think of things
that we could do
there's not a lot
an that is true

At school could not
read could not write
and left at twelve
no job in sight

In Liverpool
work hard to find
to kids like me
it was a bind

So telling lies
was one way out
became fourteen
without a doubt

And got a job
very next day
twelve bob a week
very first pay

AGE

Age can sneak up on you
turn round and it is there
some things are hard to do
nothing at all to fear

Retired some time ago
and always lots to do
many things put aside
are sure to see me through

Going grey ls normal
the body slowing down
telling us to ease up
energy can't be found

Find a chair curl up in
recall the years you spent
working hard day and night
did the job did it right

DESTINY TAKE MY HAND

Destiny Destiny
you take my hand
and lead me to
an eastern land
where people pray
five times a day
for God has said
this is the way
destiny destiny
you hold the keys
will I make it
and win the fame
or will fail
be full of shame
life can be tough
I've heard it said
done it again
fell out of bed

WHO ARE YOU

He's fairly new
round about two
can hear and see
what your up too
what's the work
what does it do
and come to that
who are you
know's your voice
sees you around
then fall asleep
well I'll be bound

A STROLL

Can I stroll down
memory lane
see the good times
just once again

Enjoy laughter
join in the fun
a last farewell
to every one

See Africa
in scorching heat
throughout the night
the drums will beat

To all of you
I'll say goodbye
to Africa
a tear a sigh

GHOSTS

They come and go
it's hard to know
where they are found
make little sound
houses, castles
and caves no doubt
will all recall
a ghost about
maybe they stay
just to be near
a loved one lost
who could appear
it's sad to know
the tears wont flow
and there they wait
till end of time
their sorrow could
be yours or mine

ANY BODY

The eyes miss nothing
what they see they store
into memory
for you to explore

Your legs carry you
your feet find the way
you'll always get there
be it night or day

Your heart never stops
your lungs always breath
the brain is on gaurd
when its help you need

Your body ready
to show you the way
support you through life
every single day

READY EDDIE

They called him Eddie
he was good as gold
he'd do job for you
not wait to be told

As the years went by
he became well known
and helping many
if they lived alone

But one day Eddie
was no longer there
they found his body
in shabby arm chair

His room was quite bare
his possessions none
though ready Eddie
had helped everyone

At his funeral
there were one or two
who recalled Eddie
and his good deeds too

DESTINY

It's hard to see
my destiny
I'll grab a cloud
and leave the crowd

Will be free
across the sea
It's sure to be
my destiny

A sandy shore
not asking more
the swaying palms
in someone's arms

The deep blue sea
whispers to me
this place could be
your destiny

PRAYERS

In many tongues
many places
we will ask for
special graces

A million prayers
will rise up high
caught by the wind
in darkened sky

Who will listen
to all those prayers
who will hear them
and see the tears

Maybe the wind
blow them away
prayers not be there
to save the day

So say your prayers
and have no fears
brought by the wind
to Him who cares

HURRY

We're all in a hurry
no time to stand and talk
even a short distance
we'd rather ride than walk

Everyone's the habit
to get it done quick quick
and slowness forgotten
we just give it the stick

Some folk hear the birds sing
some watch the clouds roll by
at night heavens sparkle
a brilliant starlit sky

We should all remember
today is just a day
all the things around us
will one day fade away

ALMOST SPOOKY

Writing can be easy
and sometimes it cannot
happens when a reader
wants to follow the plot

Can try and put them off
but that don't seem to work
only answer you get
why do you call it work

So go on without him
and sort my poem out
about a ghost haunting
my reader gives a shout

I like it it's spooky
where do we go from here
shake my hand disappear
this guy give me white hair

Readers eyes wide open
but where a ghost to find
did think of a castle
then reader came to mind

Get the poem sorted
both at castle midnight
It's just gone two am
reader nowhere in sight

NORTH OF BORDER

North of border
down Blackpool way
fate decided
to make my day

I met a girl
who changed my ways
I'm in reverse
I'm in a daze

We got on well
had lots of fun
more than enough
for anyone

We stick together
and wed as well
time decided
to ring the bell

It had to end
as most things do
where did I hear
that love is true

YESTERDAY

Sometimes you'll hear
an old refrain
that takes you down
memory lane

It rolls away
the ageing years
and sure enough
there will be tears

Our memory
will find a way
to live again
that yesterday

A MIRROR

Mirror tells the story
where beauty went to hide
but time had the answer
and time has never lied

The hair crowning glory
two eyes so big and blue
time and age will steal them
and nothing she can do

But mirror remembers
the beauty that has gone
knows she cant replace it
for time and age have won

IF I CALL

If I call
will you hear me
if I'm sad
will you be there

If I'm lost
will you find me
If I fall
then will you care

If I'm blind
will you lead me
will I know
that you are there

I don't know
all the answers
if your there
I'll have no fear

Love is blind
I've heard it said
show me where
that I should tread

OLD AGE

Old age can catch you
even though your wise
it can be sneaky
give you big surprise

Stairs have got steeper
and walks shorter foo
energy lacking
some things you can't do

Never thought you'd wear out
always full of beans
you say can do it
brain say in your dreams

Old age a blessing
feet up time is right
had good run through life
time to say goodnight

KIDS

If kids at play
keep out the way
place upside down
and stay that way

And all they need
a cardboard box
where they will hide
till someone knocks

All shoes and boots
are tried on too
they stagger round
and laugh at you

This is their world
a special one
and far too soon
it will be gone

NO RETURN

To the end of life
we will wend our way
and no one ready
to accept that day

Your time has elapsed
it's full stop for plans
and the skills you had
working with both hands

Memory fading
and thoughts not too clear
your no longer you
life will disappear

Memories friendships
and all that you knew
alas no longer
are a part of you

Who knows where you went
God alone knows why
maybe someone saw
your spirit go by

THE CORONA VIRUS

The Corona virus
will echo down the years
bringing death to thousands
and many many tears

The whole world infected
it took no time to fall
isolation needed
medics must cover all

Some countries will lock down
let nothing in or out
and cruise ship passengers
infected carried out

Our world is on knife edge
for ways to beat this foe
only time will help them
to make the virus go

ONLY YOU

And only you
can see me through
the mist of time
that split us two

And only you
can understand
and hold my hand
you used to do

And only you
roll back the years
forget the tears
you can be true

And only you
will stand by me
together be
eternally

LIBERTY

There comes a time
you've done it all
and no surprise
that you recall

You just don't care
what's next in store
you've tackled worse
and that's for sure

Good and bad times
may come and go
just forget them
don't want to know

It's often said
best things are free
and number one
is liberty

MY WORLD

Come into my world
make yourself at home
you will be welcome
always on my own

Then we could spend time
talk about the past
never stays the same
yesterday not last

When the sun goes down
count colours with me
and find the north star
it twinkles you'll see

Moonlight is gentle
caresses your hair
welcome to my world
these things you can share

LOVE IS

Never too old
to find pure gold
that's what true love is

Surprised you'll be
immediately
lucky you can be

A whispered word
a first kiss shared
in your arms she'll be

TIME

Time waits for no one
echoes down the years
and visits us all
with good news or tears

We can't avoid it
it measures our days
its the spark of life
in a million ways

We all have the time
to see our life through
but things can go wrong
and less time for you

Treat it with respect
and you'll get on fine
live life together
with your precious time

HOLIDAY

We all need
a holiday
to relax
and unwind
so we should
plan a start
before we fall apart

P AND Q

Went in search of something
it very hard to find
It's called peace and quiet
for then I could unwind

People have their problems
they can be big or small
find a quiet corner
and just forget them all

Doesn't pay to worry
the answers not around
drop into that armchair
a long long way from sound

MAYBE TOMORROW

Tomorrow is not here
it could be miles away
so you can put things off
or find another way

Happy way of dodging
when you are not quite sure
polite sort of promise
that can imply much more

Tomorrow the future
where even dreams come true
maybe you'll be lucky
and there be one for you

DO YOUR DUTY

Across the deserts
and over the seas
is a quiet life
that can only please

But this is a dream
that will not come true
the problems we have
we have to see through

Enough is enough
you can't turn your back
they call it duty
so get back on track

Yet there's only you
who knows what to do
so just get stuck in
you'll come shinning through

MEMORIES

Memories are precious
don't let them fade away
the dreary of your life
recorded every day

NOT ALONE

And some alone
will have no home
promises made
easily fade
will settle down
in any town
any doorway
there I'll stay
curl up and dream
another scene
where those I knew
would care for you
midnight is nigh
the world goes by
we're not alone
the street is home

DREAMLAND

Know a place called dreamland
it's off the beaten track
now and then I go there
and often I go back

All the things you wanted
enough to make you sigh
dreams you had forgotten
and those that make you cry

First toys ever played with
and first girl ever kissed
girl I fell in love with
who I sincerely missed

A DREAM

A long time ago
at the dead of night
I awoke from sleep
and was full of fright

As a quiet voice
in the dark bedroom
said I must promise
your time will be soon

And there wide awake
and so full of fear
who gave that message
it not at all clear

I do not feel ill
and had done no wrong
so why that message
that I've not got long

And then I went out
fresh air do me good
then heard bells ringing
in my neighbourhood

I got home and found
house burnt to the ground
remembered message
should not be around

KNOCK

One day knock on my door
but I just wont be there
will have gone forever
but only God knows where

Lived as long as I could
known good and nasty times
don't regret the journey
but tried to toe the lines

Been as fair as I could
mistakes I must have made
let the side down sometimes
a sinner I'm afraid

But few of us perfect
and far too young to earn
in back streets of city
hard for a kid to learn

Doubt that I am special
or missed by anyone
so knock and remember
that I've already gone

IT'S GONE

Gone is the summer
gone is the wine
gone is the freedom
that i thought was mine

How did I lose it
very hard to say
kindness a habit
kindness made me pay

Guess I can sort it
following the rule
when you fall in love
just another fool

FLOWERS

Flowers on arrival
and flowers when you go
a token of kindness
from all the friends you know

There at celebrations
and there at weddings too
when your life is over
they'll say goodbye to you

Many scents and colours
so quiet and serene
say the things you cannot
complete the perfect scene

A CHILD

As a child I wondered
in and out of my life
every thing I wanted
was ever out of sight

We very poor family
no wages coming in
found imagination
put problems in the bin

An eight year old dreamer
shop windows I would love
all this as good as mine
imagination time

I wanted for nothing
though had no toys at all
my imagination
would take care of it all

HOME IS IN THE DISTANCE

Home is in the distance
and not too far away
for years thought I had one
it never there to stay

Many things collected
from near and far away
nothing stayed together
it all drifted away

But the lands and places
all OK for a while
fate not in a good mood
and on me never smile

Then the storm clouds gathered
the wind blown home away
so I'll keep looking
bound to find it one day

SPARKLE

I know a story
happened long ago
friend met a Martian
would not let her go

Her name was Sparkle
wore fantastic clothes
sparkled all over
now the tears showed

She almost human
a beauty for sure
I had to help her
make it home once more

I set Sparkle free
she spread arms out wide
said friend if need me
call I'm by your side

Spun off into night
quickly out of sight
straight up to North Star
so brilliant and bright

A BUTTERFLY

To fall in love
a simple thing
a butterfly
it's on the wing

Lovely colours
gentle ways
heart will follow
maybe it stays

You hold it tight
it flies no more
love and beauty
lay on the floor

MY STAR

There is a star
that knows me well
it always knows
just where I dwell

At eventide
I search the sky
and sure enough
it sparkles high

And deep in sleep
it's there for me
my star and I
good company

YOUR BODY

Your body runs
on food and drink
you have a brain
can also think

The eyes and brain
can sort it out
all your problems
without a doubt

The body knows
when your not well
high temperature
so you can tell

The best machine
you'll ever meet
it runs for years
now that's a treat

ALERT

We'd best look out
a bug about
dodgy weather
stick together

Six feet apart
a yard or two
it's good advice
for all of you

The NHS
is on the ball
well backed up
must cover all

Its tough for all
and worse for some
with loved ones lost
by everyone

YOUR STAR

If you care
will you be there
then we're together

All alone
I'm on my own
long way from home

Thoughts of you
will trickle through
the good times we knew

We'll unite
both out of sight
home in our starlight

A SONG

Long ago far away
deep in the mist of time
heard an angel singing
melody that was mine

High and low it wandered
in and out of the cloud
stars sparkled above me
an audience so proud

Her song now a murmur
end this fantastic show
figure of the angel
now just a gentle glow

HOPE

Hope a good companion
so don't lose sight of him
always there on your side
in with a chance to win

True that life a gamble
we all can win or lose
hope is there to help you
so how can you refuse

Must be optimistic
and hope is all you need
won't solve all your problems
but good chance you'll succeed

A PROBLEM

Seem to have a problem
just don't know right from wrong
when I tend to let go
then someone comes along

Taps me on the shoulder
says you know this is wrong
I find life straight forward
and never puzzled long

Could I stray get away
I don't think it would cost
just tapped on the shoulder
told home before your lost

SOMEWHERE

Hard to understand
cruel some can be
take away your home
your security

Leave you with nothing
income very low
you are unsteady
no one wants to know

No bed to sleep in
and no fire to warm
a winters morning
life can be forlorn

Too old start again
I don't give in
somewhere a future
where I will fit in

THE RAILWAY

A railway man
I used to be
in a signal box
my duty
check train traffic
too and fro
me a bobby that is so

TO GO

We go on a journey
to a distant star
long long time to get there
it's very very far

For earth now unstable
explosions day and night
war broke out all over
and people want to fight

Bombs affect the weather
there's floods and storms each day
back to normal never
we have to go away

Took some time to plan it
and help from those who knew
kind of transport needed
and where to get a crew

Money not a problem
and fifty keen to go
well mixed group of people
and others want to know

Our new hone like the Earth
it has a sun and moon
oxygen and water
plus lots and lots of room

And now all set to go
we'll let our people know
off we go tomorrow
and don't look back just go

Transport in forest
away from prying eyes
then crew fired rockets
and launched us to the skies

Into orbit we go
and speeding into space
the earth a tiny ball
and tears on every face

DELICATE CREATURES

Girls can be a problem
as we wander through life
throw their arms around you
or chase you out of sight

Never quite sure of them
there temperamental too
think you've got them sorted
there I be no chance for you

Girls delicate creatures
that more or less is true
only carry hand bags
might hold a brick or two

So girlfriend protect you
and worth her weight in gold
sort out all the bad guys
and knock them out stone cold

ON THE RAILS 4472

Lots to do
have no fear
nothing lost
keep you safe
every day
what more
can I say

TO DO

To do what you want
to say what you feel
to follow the flow
and live life for real

To hear what they say
to fine there's a way
and day after day
you can hope and pray

To look at the past
to find it wont last
for time goes so fast
It's too late to ask

BEAUTY-A WOMAN'S PRIDE

Beauty a woman's pride
her hair crowning glory
time will take this away
leave different story

Age you can get used to
and take things as they come
and take our time to work
don't do it on the run

A woman loves her beauty
and to be sure her hair
she I notice in mirror
it's sadly gone but where

STAN

I once met a man
called secondhand Stan
he said this was true
he owned nothing new

He lived alone
in his secondhand home
disliked spending too
so his friends were few

He said old things last
well made in the past
some thought him mean
not at market seen

Then one day Stan died
council got with pride
Stan's box of cash
to help all who ask

LAST YEAR

The year has gone
and took someone
that I knew well
but should not dwell
the past is past
and will not last
memory may
just pave the way
and let you stay
with yesterday

FAITH

Religion can be all
for many people call
on their god to help them
when life has brought a fall

We all have our problems
and we all have our fears
faith is part of our life
when we can't stop the tears

We on top of mountain
or in a prison cell
faith will know there's someone
that someone you can tell

Our world turns around us
there's galaxies in space
we all have our problems
must meet them face to face

HIJACKED TO MARS

If you look far
your sure to see
a place they call
eternity

It's said we all
will end up there
if good or bad
so have no fear

Will stay be long
or stay be short
have this feeling
that I've been caught

Many people
are gathered here
yet it too quiet
could it be fear

Got this feeling
I need a lift
it's only one girl
who has that gift

Whisper Sparkle
can you come down
she stands beside me
and with a frown

She shakes her head
and grabs my arm
then we spin off
before alarm

Very distant
and very far
they call it Mars
the red star

The red planet
I've seen in space
Sparkle from Mars
so full of grace

FRIENDLY FREDDY COULD NOT READ

I heard a story
hard to believe
about a ghost
that could not read

And St Peter
would let him free
help improve
his a b c

Friendly Freddy
has spent much time
in the bookshops
library fine

Need to notice
so that I know
the way to talk
and say hello

Friendly Freddy
sometimes he found
that both his feet
not on the ground

People noticed and
and got a shock
see right through him
about a block

He found it hard
looked in mirror
said this must end
look a terror

Found some clothes on
a washing line
looked in mirror
said this do fine

Friendly Freddy
works in book shop
St Peter pleased
he talks like a toff

THE NIGHT TRAIN

A lonely call
that's meant for me
the midnight train
of memory

It knows the way
it takes me back
along the years
and down the track

The past rolls out
before your eyes
to memory
its no surprise

That lonely call
whistled again
you can't forget
the midnight train

RAIL TRIP

Sometimes fancy
a railroad run
every chance to have some fun
clickety click
the wheels go around
were on our way
we'll I'll be bound

A RING

To have and to hold
a ring made of gold
our future untold
our life will unfold

It's not always true
the future and you
whatever you do
can break up us two

Can try as you may
every single day
just cant find a way
the right words to say

THE RIGHT ROAD

If you know the right road
then follow it to the end
you'll know where you going
and know what's round the bend

Life can give surprises
with good or bad effect
but your ready for them
it's something you expect

As your growing older
there's chances you might take
right road takes you round them
so you make no mistake

FRIENDLY FREDDY

Book shop busy
Freddy need help
put lots of books
up on the shelf

The book shop boss
said need more staff
two or three more
would fill the gap

Friendly Freddy
said got some friends
St Peter yes
then good help send

St Peter not
sure if it sane
that more spirits
should go again

Permission gained
at very top
the three girls could
work at the shop

Mil Til and Jane
had to do same
walk through doorways
not the walls please

Keep feet on floor
when in the shop
never ever
float round the shop

The girls looked down
we look a mess
can we go to
your M and S

Freddy had frown
no go to town
charity shop
will dress you down

The shop is closed
Freddy says do
what always do
walk through the wall

The girls sorted
a lot of gear
so very nice
they would appear

The girls next day
wore doing fine
boss said Freddy
your a gold mine

Freddy puzzled
not understand
boss said girls OK
and shook his hand

THOUGHTS

Sometimes my thoughts wonder
at life in other lands
a day out in China
a stroll on some strange sands

Then I could make a start
along the China wall
and then off to Egypt
give pyramids a call

And see Easter island
it's statues mystery
they still stare silently
so far across the sea

Walk the skeleton coast
score of shipwrecks to see
the sands have a secret
for diamonds there may be

A RACE

Out of this world
a big surprise
a million stars
before your eyes

Galaxy's there
we cannot count
colours galore
and much much more

Distance is great
telescopes see
fantastic worlds
infinitely

Yet tiny earth
could win the race
humanity
could set the pace

A RIVER

Moonlight on the river
that carry's you and me
sparkles and gleaming
into eternity

The moonlight is magic
as the waves come and go
on the river of life
a river we well know

We both know the sunshine
we both know the rain
the storms will come and go
but there's sunshine again

Life may be a river
if so don't be too sad
many many good things
and very few that's bad

FISH AND CHIPS

Fish and chips
I love to eat
when I'm hungry
they are a treat
other food
I often scoff
but fish and chips
are at the top

DREAMING

I'm not long for this world
I'm hurrying to the next
ain't got time to dawdle
and ain't got time to text

Everybody rushing
and where to I don't know
when I get a minute
then I'll go for a blow

Maybe there's a sale on
St Peters at the door
have you got a ticket
I said whatever for

WEARY

The load is heavy
and the road is steep
all you can think of
is a long long sleep

That is for many
the easy way out
duty we all have
so we turn about

Just stick to the road
and those you care for
wont increase the load
to final abode

THE SPIRIT

Friends and loved ones
people you know
do you ever
think where they go

Some are religious
and some are not
so where are they
at life's full stop

Eternity
they would now know
disappointed
possibly so

It is the end
if spirit gone
spirit special
have only one

A LIE

Tell A Porky
can be naughty
but sometimes save the day
might stop a tear
from someone dear
when you cant find a way

A ROAD

We all have a road
and tread it each day
all are different
so don't lose your way

Some of us lucky
and some of us not
cant predict future
just take what you've got

Many things guide you
securely through life
make sure you get there
and avoid the strife

A LANE

It will be the same
it could be a game
just memory lane

Whatever you say
you'll find yesterday
different no way

Spend time in the past
find love that did last
but time goes so fast

We all have this book
at it's pages look
what yesterday took

LOST

Don't leave me alone
to find my way home
the journey is long
the road may be wrong

I could lose my way
the clouds come to stay
can't see through the mist
so long since we kissed

Just an old arm chair
that we used to share
together at last
two lost in the past

YOUR HEART

Heart is special
in every way
many duties
no time to play

Heart an engine
drive you through life
will know good times
will know the strife

So look after
that special part
your hard working
and faithful heart

THE JOURNEY

The journey is hard
but travel you must
there is no reward
but on us it's thrust

Some find it easy
and some find it hard
as they make their way
and count every yard

Life is different
for those who are bright
but many struggle
and find life a fight

All of us get there
and find in the end
that no one knows
what lies round the bend

EYES OF MEMORY

Eyes are very special
they notice everything
what they saw yesterday
will be well recorded
carefully filed away
memory there for you
will never make you wait
eyes have not forgot them
they will recall the date

GOD

Who will ask the question
and who will tell you why
searched and searched for God
yet he may be close by

Heavens wide and open
and nowhere he could hide
space is all around us
nowhere he could abide

Maybe in a rainbow
or early morning sun
or after a hard day
and thank God that is done

Perhaps it's the spirit
that's inside everyone
never ever thought of
but there till we are gone

NO RETURN JOURNEY

245

The road is long
there is no song
that you could sing
or anything

That tells you why
a darkened sky
the day has gone
you where someone

You futures where
somewhere out there
and round the bend
we'll find the end

Our journey done
and then we learn
the road we tread
has no return

THANK GOD

There is a time
we are alone
be anywhere
could be your home

And God not there
that we can see
and then again
He just may be

He hears your prayers
and what you ask
and few it is
who share His task

But always there
for us to ask
in the future
and in the past

MY ANGEL

I follow the wind
searching for my love
the strangest places
fit her like a glove

And ancient Egypt
history sore
pyramid whisper
there is so much more

China India
and Everest too
don't think anywhere
that she's not been to

When she spreads her wings
I just can't say no
her world is outside
so she has to go

Know I'll be sorry
I've run out of luck
for she wont be here
when I do wake up

GONE TO DUST

Hard to talk of death
voice no longer there
never to call you
thoughts no longer share

Full stop to future
also yesterday
no more tomorrows
whatever you say

Good times remembered
bad times forget
always memory
and have no regret

TAKE TIME

Take time to recall
of just where you are
neighbours so distant
from our tiny star

Yet planets and worlds
around us abound
but no place like earth
in space can be found

Still we go in search
and one day will see
that elusive star
earths sister must be

MAYBE

We all have a choice
it yes or no
all must decide
it come or go

All must agree
the answer we choose
is it a winner
or likely to lose

It could be tricky
it got to be done
a war or woman
would never be won

Lucky dips not on
or spinning a dime
to yourself be true
make your mind up time

WOULD I COULD I

Would I could I
make dreams come true
would I could I
hold on to you

You disappeared
one moonlit night
gone forever
out of my sight

River river
you must know more
where she went to
what foreign shore

Rippling waters
they seem to say
love comes and goes
that is the way

FATE AND FACT

There is a time
there is a place
meet the future
Fate to face

And tell him
we toed the line
followed orders
been on time

Fate shakes his head
and says you tried
and many times
tears I cried

Your on the edge
and push your luck
but got to admit
you've got pluck

RHODESIA THE HOME

In Rhodesia
settled down
lots of work
to be found
can do most
with lots of work
soon build a home
then relax we not alone

TO BE ALONE

To be alone
it is no shame
many people
will be the same

Companionship
is good for you
must be steady
and must be true

Friends can be great
and good to know
sincerity
what they must show

WHEN ITS GONE

When its gone its gone
it could be your life
or something you learn
not always able
to sail through the storm
you end up alone
and very forlorn
your life cant be held
or put on a lead
no one is able
to alter the speed
yet we rush through life
and find that we know
some are successful
and many not so

PROBLEMS

Got problems for breakfast
and problems for tea
if some don't get sorted
don't know where I'll be

Lots and lots of people
tell you what to do
have they got the answer
no not got a clue

Go through life best you can
mistakes by the score
you will find that no one
will open every door

Got to find your own way
down the street of life
don't know what's round the bend
if fate out of sight

A PICTURE

Walking through the trees
silver birches please
river splashes by
wind to give a sigh
walk into the mist
a mystery for all
its just a picture
hanging on the wall

SPARKLE IN SPACE

I hear the beat
is it my heart
will it tell me
must be apart

Your not of earth
and hard to find
and love your life
the Martian kind

Guess I'll stargaze
every night
and watch for you
to come in sight

Sparkle sparkle
my special star
you can hear me
however far

So speed your way
into my arms
with all your sparkle
and Martian charms

WHERE IN WONDERLAND

Many roads to travel
and many miles to go
will I find you waiting
or is that just not so

Patience and tears
together no harm
hoping you will be there
and free me from alarm

The years have taken
the sparkle from your eyes
when we are together
will be a big surprise

Build the home you wanted
exactly as you planned
then remain together
within our wonderland

A DREAM OF NOWHERE

Know a place called nowhere
it's almost out of sight
quiet as the country
where people never fight

Everybody friendly
I'm sure this can't be right
sunshine every morning
and moonlight every night

So next time I go there
I'll check it on the map
ideal place to drop off
especially for a nap

FATE

Time will get you places
trust time to get you there
maybe best you dawdle
and be late everywhere

If you never on time
and if your always late
your future erratic
and a head ache to fate

Most folk are clock watchers
and all do things on time
your never there when should be
but live a long long time

IS THERE

Is there a future
that's waiting for me
or is it no more
I'm likely to be

A question that's asked
and many that do
found none comes back
to give us a clue

I guess its too hard
to think were no more
our life has gone out
and closes the door

There's so many things
that had meant to do
now impossible
to sort that lot through

So please remember
fate can't send a card
he's far too busy
but will beg your pard

THE FUTURE QUESTIONS

All questions and answers
this simple life we heed
everybody curious
where it's going to lead

Some of us will progress
while others have it tough
for who and what you are
may not be quite enough

The future is special
for no one knows what's there
understand it's hidden
can't find it anywhere

Good or bad one day know
and patience is the thing
cannot dodge the future
and it may have a sting

Cannot find the future
be happy here on earth
do what you do well
be glad you born on earth

LIFE WE SPEND

We all have a beginning
and we all have an end
and it's up to fate
how long the life we spend

Some of us are lucky
and will reach high old age
others die in childhood
and some in their schooldays

Accidents and illness
will also take their toll
cannot dodge the column
if we are on fates roll

ETERNITY

Was once asked a question
about eternity
and what I would do there
when it was time for me

Not an easy answer
for no one has returned
I don't think you go there
so that much you have learned

Heaven if your lucky
you will find here on earth
hell a part of your life
so give it a wide birth

OUR WORLD A GIFT

Our world a gift from the gods
and earth a special place
mountains deserts forests
like nowhere else in space

Our sun controls plant life
our moon controls the tides
fruit and fish plentiful
our oceans deep and wide

Many animals here
and lots of crops we grow
a peaceful place to be
to war we would say no

Not always the answer
we've idiots for sure
hell bent on destruction
a danger to be sure

DREAM OF NITA

Dreams never come true
but out of the blue
fell in love with you
Nita

And puzzled when I
see tears in your eye
and ask myself why
Nita

One day I will go
to Ireland you know
then your tears will flow
Nita

May have grown older
love can be bolder
my arms enfold her
Nita

QUESTIONS

Many folk ask questions
and many like the truth
some things hard too answer
and those who know aloof

All things have beginning
and all things have an end
this could be a lifetime
where all their way will wend

All a varied future
depending on your birth
good luck may surround you
throughout your life on Earth

We all make the journey
it can be long or short
back to earth our mother
from which we once came forth

FUTURES DOOR

Is it too late
to catch that dream
escaped before
not to be seen

About the time
I got it right
I'm in clover
success in sight

And sad to say
it did not last
that leap forward
now in the past

Not beaten yet
try futures door
it may be open
at last I'll score

WHISPERING SANDS

There's a story
and there's a land
known by the wind
whispering sands

And all that's gone
sand will recall
the lakes and forests
the mountains tall

Animals there
and people too
then frozen world
and none lived through

Wind shook his head
and gave a sigh
that long ago
now you and I

HYPERMARKETS – SOUTH AFRICA

Sold Everything
in large quantities
Sugar twenty pounds a bag
tea and coffee the same
flour and fruit
you had a bigger trolley
a cheaper price
and small you look for

A DREAMING

Dreaming in the rain
guess it is a shame
never meet again
and I wonder why

Had so much to say
somewhere lost the way
and parted that day
always makes me sigh

Could we meet again
would it be the same
time alone to blame
broke up you and I

NO TOMORROW

Don't need tomorrow
I'm going nowhere
would be a waste of time
those I know not there

Life does not need them
they have gone away
give up the struggle
and called it a day

Life is a journey
we find our way through
the answer may be
those who cared for you

HAPPINESS

Happiness we look for
but never always find
could be something simple
or an act that was kind

Life can cheer you up
but also let you down
none of us is perfect
you never on them frown

Happiness is children
just playing in a street
everyone's a stranger
with a smile they all greet

EVENING

The darkness is here
daylight ran away
where did it go to
no one can say

Some clouds hide the moon
the stars want to shine
sprinkle their beauty
both your way and mine

Beautiful picture
quiet and serene
not always noticed
and not always seen

NEVER LOOK BACK

Never look back
yesterdays gone
so don't waste time
tomorrows come

We all recall
things from the pstt
just remember
they did not last

And many thoughts
will cross your mind
you remember
those who were kind

Life can be short
don't waste a day
your tomorrow
far far away

TRAVELLING

I like to do
but that was
when I was
when I
twenty two
now getting
old and grey
yes it was yesterday

CHOICE

Your life has many roads
so which one will you pick
will it be the fast one
that gets you there quite quick

Then again the slow road
that lets you stand and stare
think about your future
and the people there

True we all have choices
they can be good or bad
on your journey through life
sometimes they will be sad

INTO EACH LIFE

Into each life
some rain must fall
unlucky you
you've got it all

If things go wrong
the blame you get
if they go right
they soon forget

Mistakes a habit
I've made a lot
make a fortune
alas I'll not

HAUNTED HEART

Thought I heard you singing
down corridor of time
voice was ringing
melody that was mine

Always in the distance
a long long way from me
in dreams the only place
where you and me can be

Haunt my dreams forever
our worlds far apart
never go forever
you left a haunted heart

TIME STANDS STILL

I sometimes think
that time stands still
and as a boy
I have no will
to join others
who in their teens
just have no time
for childish scenes
but I'm happy
when here or home
alas always
just on my own

A TRAVELLER

Somewhere across a sea
of stars waiting for me
I'll find my dream of dreams
who sought infinity

She would travel through space
and never lose her way
but time was a close friend
who would show her the way

Such beautiful colours
and worlds so far apart
for she loved the silence
it was this touched her heart

She seems more of a ghost
in my dreams when we meet
my galaxy traveller
who one day I will greet

DRIVING

Driving I like
and done my bit
as an airman
I trained for it
always happy
at the wheel
take you anywhere
that's a deal

A HEART

Heart is a worker
and not a shirker
it just pumps your blood
the work that it does

Goes on day and night
so never lose sight
as heart works for you
a duty to do

Through hail rain and snow
it ensures you go
and be there on time
you and your heart fine

NO AFRICAN TWILIGHT

There's no twilight
dawn at five am
dark at six pm
the day goes by
a cloudless sky
a spring and summer
no winter
the stars at night
the Milky Way
is on display
but far far away

LOOK

Look into the future
something we cannot do
always best avoided
see good and bad come true

To know what will happen
and look before it does
lay heavy on your mind
just as a secret does

So few seek the future
the good times come and go
bad times they will happen
till then don't want to know

A BRAIN

Brain has got the answer
to every question asked
it wont always tell you
a secret that should last

For brain knows your body
and regulates your life
listens to your heart beat
and never give you fright

So brain will never sleep
got far too much to do
night and day on duty
ensuring you are you

ALWAYS DREAMING

Dreaming always dreaming
and one day they'll come true
you'll be here beside me
my one and only you

Words are not the answer
and rings are not secure
love alone can bond us
it opens every door

I'll never forget you
though time thrust us apart
I'll hold you once again
feel the beat of your heart

GIRLS

Most girls are strange
and hard to know
if they like you
they'll tell you so

Find they trust you
welcome you near
secrets well kept
nothing to fear

Make a partner
guide you through life
last but not least
a perfect wife

I DREAM OF PLACES

Lots of places
I want to be
around the world
many to see

Where it's quiet
and hear birds sing
gentle raindrops
touch everything

The sky above
a sparkling blue
and the sunset
has gold for you

Lots of places
I'd like to see
so come along
and dream with me

SOUTH AFRICA DRIVE-IN

Liked
the drive-in's
a big screen
two films
get fish and chips there
all into our pickup
two hours fun
cost two Rand a quid

A LIFE

No one lives forever
it may or not be true
we all have a measure
if short or long to do

Long life can be happy
or full of ups and downs
should never be squandered
or scattered on the ground

Many ways to use it
the choice is up to you
so trust you'll be lucky
travel the long road through

LIFE IS TOO SHORT

Life is too short
to squander a day
not get it back
whatever you pay

Most watch the clock
in so many ways
doing their best
to stretch their days

Time does not stop
and waits for no one
time has no clock
give all a shock

CAREFUL WITH A WISH

Be careful if you wish
because it may come true
be at the rainbows end
nothing at all to do

You don't need a future
and you don't need a past
got years and years to go
but then again you asked

You want life to stop
get richer every day
and friends are growing older
yet you don't grow that way

Money troubles no more
it's to be secure
but sometimes I wonder
is my future no more

TOMORROW NEVER COMES

They say tomorrow
never comes
but we know it does
be ready

So you don't get caught
tomorrow
could be worth a thought
too easy

Saying I don't care
why worry
what will be will be
fingers crossed

Will probably do
worked for me
and it should for you
give it a thought

LONG GONE

There it was at last
though faint from the past
a gentle gasp
but her

And hard to recall
go hoped would not fall
I would loose all
for her

It' so long ago
since she said hello
thought love always grow
but no

Now she's just a dream
no where to be seen
the world was our scene
no more

STRAY FROM HOME

There's many ways
to stray from home
never ever
stray alone
all your treasures
you've put by
you give to them
a last goodbye

ROAD THROUGH LIFE

There is a road
that we must take
and no mistake
wander off it
and you will find
not every one
the pleasant kind
our world is full
of good and bad
and many sights
that make you sad
and then again
around the bend
world of colour
sunset to end
your road though life

AFRICA WHERE MY HEART IS

Been around
there's lots
to see
the sun
all day
and nights
sultry
warmer than UK
where my heart is

WHERE WE KNOW NOWT

Many people
including me
don't know nowt
about eternity
is it a place
or not at all
just a figment
that we recall
that futures gone
the past also
maybe it's time
to just let go
so many things
that we don't know

RHODESIA OVER

Rhodesia
is history
a diamond
in the sun
alas her days
are over
almost before
they begun
Cecil Rhodes empire
fought
but did not win

MARS

I steal through the night
my heart beat thunder
the world out of sight
just gliding through space

Where is the north star
it's light will guide me
till I see clearly
the red planet Mars

For there is a friend
that taught me to wander
not fear the thunder
of red planet Mars

MAYBE IN THE FUTURE

Look beyond the sunset
to find a brand new world
then we can discover
a mystery unfurled

Will we ever find it
or is it just a dream
where folks never battle
where killing is obscene

Religion greed terror
no longer rules the world
the day when we find it
a mystery unfurled

LIFE IN THE FUTURE

We all have a future
and we all have a past
we weave our way through life
who knows if it will last

Some of us are lucky
the world is at their feet
others struggle daily
and hope that both ends meet

The same wide world over
have and have nots are there
good fortune uneven
so many in despair

Sometimes warlike nations
and sometimes greed it's true
as soldiers come and steal
your land away from you

A SECRET

The stars have the answer
but they will never tell
the sun and moon this secret
have known for aeons as well
earth alone in darkness
no one allowed to tell

WHAT IS ETERNITY

What is eternity
is it a place for all
do we travel from there
or is it our last call

Good and bad together
or some that went before
some nice folk have gone there
and killers by the score

Can be just a question
of how you lived your life
find heaven here on earth
and hell is out of sight

CAN'T SAY NO

No if's or butts
when you go you go
can't pull no strings
or look other way
so lets face it
we cant run away
lots made the trip
but they don't come back
or give a tip
so no road back
I see St Peter
who leans on the gate
has a great big smile
and says your late

THE FUTURE A SECRET

Futures are secret
and we'll never know
what can await us
wherever we go

It could be success
or making the grade
or just second class
and well in the shade

Life full of errors
mistakes to be made
what you do do well
and don't be afraid

FATE AGAIN

Fate misses nothing
you can't hide from him
turn up anywhere
none expecting him

He has a duty
and follows the rules
will help the wise one
and comfort the fools

The cause he must see
and cannot be late
you'll never be missed
on a date with Fate

A WISH UPON A STAR

If I wished upon a star
would it get me very far
could speed off into space
look around some other place

Lots of planets round about
trifle cold I have no doubt
Mars I like so I'll go there
caves to shelter in I hear

Took me ages very red
so find the caves into bed
next day had a look around.
lots of stuff from earth I found

In the distance earth I see
it looks strange and quite tiny
planets got a lot to see
hope I make it home for tea

BEAUTY FOR TODAY

Beauty for today
for it will not stay
and will always go
to your special show
down memory lane

LIFE A QUESTION

Often asked the question
and all I gives a sigh
I don't know the answer
so they pass me by

Life and death hereafter
will need some time for thought
some not like the answer
it's not quite what they sought

Many forms of worship
are practised here on earth
each one gives peace of mind
and guarantees it's worth

Everyone different
and choose their way through life
avoiding the problems
and avoiding the strife

If the heart stops beating
impossible to breath
the brain will not function
and life our body leave

HELLO TOMORROW

Hello tomorrow
and where have you been
just hiding away
don't want to be seen

Your bringing good news
or will it be bad
I don't take a chance
presume it will be sad

I trust what you say
a job to be done
some will be happy
and some will be glum

NUMBER ONE

We don't know our future
and that's how it should be
worries enough to sort
to dwell on what might be

Life is full of problems
and tackled one by one
so your sure to get there
by slowly plodding on

The hard times will stress you
but you must carry on
many depend on you
for your their number one

RIVER OF LIFE

A life is a river
that takes you out to sea
day born your bewildered
for all a mystery

And then you get older
your world you've got to know
a million and one things
just got to have a go

To seek out the mountains
and the jungles galore
to visit strange countries
stand on a foreign shore

Mum and dad wonder too
where on earth you got to
nose deep in travel book
library's special nook

YOU CAN

You can be specific
and sail the pacific
that's where the trade winds blow
then it's easy to reach
find a palm shaded beach
always wanted to know

THE BANKERS CAT

The bankers cat
has thick black fur
investigates all
who steps in here
he's on the staff
so have no fear
everyone is welcome here
he likely has
expensive meals
unlike most cats
he never steals
sees business sorted
by the score
you couldn't really
ask for more
than a lucky black cat
at the bankers door

A LONELY MEMORY

May be unkind
to bare in mind
a memory alone
we leave behind
of times we shared
with those who cared
never ever alone

A BOND

Loose a mothers love
so where will you be
in a dark tunnel
no light will you see

Can't find the answer
nothing we can do
where is forgiveness
none is left for you

Maybe in future
there's a tear or two
blown away by wind
all that's left of you

MEMORY IS GONE

It may not seem fair
but we all get there
the end of the line
when there's no more time

Memory is gone
a lot more than one
just nothing to do
it cannot be you

And where have I gone
me the only one
so it must be true
your no longer you

RAINING IN MY HEART

Why did we have to part
our future did not start
just raining in my heart

And love is hard to find
true life can be unkind
have you made up your mind

Just dancing with you
and I'd never be blue
recall your first hello

That was long long ago
your love and also mine
gone with the wind and time

MEMORIES TO HOLD

To have and to hold
always there for you
so fresh and so true
just turn the clock back
a surprise for you
she's not changed at all
eyes sparkle and blue
how did she get there
far away from you
a mass of gold hair
and sparkling blue eyes
light up in surprise
when we meet again
in memory lane

OLD GOLD

It will be old
definitely gold
the memory
we treasured

Of times long gone
far more than one
when we were close
and together

Just give your eyes
a big surprise
and realise
dreams come true

THE IMPOSSIBLE

You can climb a mountain
you can weather the storm
do the impossible
and that's why you were born

We have conquered all things
some difficult to do
always win the challenge
it can be tough for you

Some will have the courage
while other look for fame
to all it's a challenge
they've got to win the game

LOOK IN THE FUTURE

Look in the future
and what do I see
end of the world
where I like to be

I have done most things
and strange places seen
and followed the rules
wherever they've been

The road to nowhere
I'll tread to the end
and follow the crowd
the future will send

GOD KNOWS

Seems wars are forever
despite a bloody past
we are learning slowly
and surely peace will last

Can we find the answer
and all destruction cease
all the world hand in hand
should be praying for peace

If we never find it
our earth will spin away
destroyed by its children
and God forbid that day

FREEDOM A DREAM

Kind of in prison
prison of the mind
no one to rescue
no one to be kind

The years will go by
and I heave a sigh
but what have I done
freedom can't be won

Only seek the end
and that round the bend
the answer I found
just is not around

KNOWLEDGE

Knowledge is a good thing
so never turn it down
put you in the front row
and on it never frown

Always have the answers
know what you need to do
and if things get tricky
you can lead the way through

Knowledge help you progress
in every thing you do
always have the answers
and certain what to do

A TRIP

If you take my hand
we will leave the land
and circle the earth
leave it far below

Mars worth a look
red as you see
it can be quite old
for planet to be

Beautiful Saturn
it's fantastic rings
spinning forever
invisible wings

Such beautiful stars
but too far away
for us to visit
in a single day

So we will speed back
through our milky way
I see mother Earth
we've had a good day

THE ROAD

Life has many corners
many bends in the road
some of them can help you
and some increase your load

None can tell the future
as fate takes care of that
we all do our duty
have little time to chat

Most look after children
and guide them day by day
no thoughts for the future
they're with them every day

ROUNDABOUT

Life a roundabout
many ups and downs
often on the ups
lot more on the downs

Good news you'd hoped for
it not ever there
bad news you don't want
almost everywhere

So go with the flow
you'll make it one day
but it be likely
you'll be old and grey

LOTS OF QUESTIONS

There are lots of questions
that I would like to ask
some about the future
and some about the past

Do we have a heaven
and do we have a hell
friends no longer with us
they don't come back to tell

Religion you follow
sincerity your guide
your prayers will be personal
and faith be on your side

Religions are many
some hard to understand
only faith and worship
will see that helping hand

SOMETIMES

Sometimes I hear an old refrain
which takes me back down memory lane
a haunting lilt from out the past
surprising how the sweetness lasts
of happiness or sorrow
so different on the morrow

YOU

It's got to be
a memory
a long long time
away from me

And dreams not clear
in light of day
you disappear
what can I say

As twilight comes
will you appear
take me with you
so lonely here

SWINGS OF LIFE

Up and down swings of life
will carry us away
never know where we'll land
and who is there to say

The good times on the up
but problems on the down
none of them expected
and they'll produce a frown

Swinging high swinging low
you cannot stop the swing
nothing impossible
your future it will bring

RESEARCH

Sad sad world we live in
so many people die
so many diseases
we cannot cure but why

Lots of time and money
first class research involved
yet we search for answers
as many still unsolved

We are making progress
and living longer too
so lets all be grateful
to work researchers do

SO TIRED

Not a cheerful subject
but death welcome to some
end to all worry's
an end to pain for some

Lots of things you can't do
a good nights sleep not there
all the places you like
will never see you there

Life closing in on you
memories see you through
yesterday still quite clear
but nothing left for you

A LAD

You make your way slowly
from cradle to the grave
and the things that you learn
your memory will save

Simple things as a child
to get you safe through schools
and as you grow older
just how to handle tools

Then you start your first job
your working on your own
very proud to be there
but lonely on your own

Got that success feeling
my first days work OK
ready for the future
and roll on first weeks pay

YOUR TIME

We all have time
and throw it away
and sure enough
get a rainy day
too much to do
can't sort it out
so never ever
chuck time out

A LIFE TO CHANGE

Might change the weather
but cant change the world
like a stone you throw
land where ever hurled

Folks follow habits
and have done for years
others face hard times
and have many fears

Some will find success
every thing possess
some face a winter
of hunger distress

Cannot avoid it
life set out for you
have luck and courage
that will pull you through

SUNSET

The day is over
a coloured sky
and painted by
the suns bye bye
it's a nice way
to say goodnight
surrounded
by starlight

WHEEL OF FORTUNE

So wheel of fortune
spin my world around
show me the good times
take feet off the ground

Give me a future
that I only dream
grant all my wishes
for things that I've seen

Help me to travel
round the world non stop
how can I thank you
money I have not

So wheel of fortune
there's just one thing more
I fell out of bed
got bruises galore

OUR COLONY

Almost
at war
two tribes
want to rule
destroy Rhodes dream
Britain say talk
but us locals
we stay put

OUR MEMORY LANE

Anytime
any date
we could meet
at the gate
we could stroll
down our lane
be the same
just us two
as we were
and your long
golden hair
that sparkled
in the sun
and startled
everyone
when we meet
once again
always be
just the same
don't be late
at the gate
down our memory lane

GOOD FRIENDS

I saw a cat and a mouse
one day
and had to rub
my eyes
they never are the
best of friends
but that is no
surprise
yet these two seemed
deep in thought
and the mouse
did not seem caught
the mouse seemed to know
what is what
and told the cat
I'm all you've got
your one and only perk
so never ever catch me
or we'll both be out of work

MIDNIGHT

In the still
of the night
all quiet
then moonlight
will chase the
shadows
out of sight
spread silver
everywhere

TIME WILL NOT WAIT

Time is not forever
nothing is to last
thoughts you had yesterday
already in the past

So all you rely on
blown away in the wind
and time will not notice
because time is tough skinned

So be full of promise
time will show you the way
though time very busy
and that was yesterday

Remember your wishes
and remember your ways
and maybe you'll get there
to see those special days

SEARCHED ALONE

I've wandered far and searched alone
looking for a place called home
in many lands and many places
the scenes the same with coloured faces
even in a crowded street
never a friendly face I meet
I wonder if eternity
will be the same for such as me

STARDUST

Tears in my eyes
is no surprise
must get wise
just stardust

What can I say
no time to play
she makes my day
It's stardust

I search night sky
ask myself why
her home the sky
my stardust

SOMETIMES ITS HARD

Sometimes it's hard
to say goodbye
looking up to
a clear blue sky

You've lost someone
not see again
where have they gone
who is to blame

Death comes and goes
I give a sigh
is the answer
in that blue sky

MARILYN MONROE

Only one girl
that is for sure
work her way up
from showbiz floor
can sing and dance
and pull a tear
a brand new star
she would appear
her beauty too
a big surprise
fantastic body
that opened eyes
but at the top
fame and friends
deserted her
now Marilyn
no longer seen
good luck Marilyn
wherever you rest
still at the top
one of the best

HER

I once found her
but let her go
it was not my show
she showed love
and care for me
they stopped liberty
sometimes I hear
her voice in the wind
echoing echoing

I WANT TO GO HOME

I want to go home
wont be alone
when people will say
how goes it each day

The wind blows the corn
there where I was born
blows troubles away
what more can I say

It vanished from sight
one cold winters night
I recall the name
it was memory lane

OUR TIME

No one knows the future
yet we all like to know
are we here tomorrow
or have we had to go
no one lives forever
our body soon worn out
fate and time will tell us
our time is running out

WATCHING AGE

Age is round the corner
no one can sneak by
fate is watching closely
with an eagle eye

Bit slower every day
but memories stacked away
will enjoy again
and look at yesterday

Once again see them
though many years go by
bring a tear or two
and probably a sigh

TOGETHER

Whether together
or whether alone
we miss each other
when I'm not at home

Travel the country
a living I make
always remember
the family at stake

So cannot deny
that parted we be
soon back together
with our family

LIFE FROM THE CRADLE

From the cradle
into the grave
find time alone
is all you save

There's lots to do
and lots to see
all recorded
in memory

We get older
surprise in store
we'd have children
who could ask more

They find their way
just like you did
and make mistakes
you must forgive

Takes time to learn
and get it right
but stand your ground
and win your fight

TOMORROW IS NOT HERE

Tis said tomorrow
likes to hide away
it cannot face us all
whatever the day

No one can find it
its guilty say some
been up to mischief
can't face anyone

Seems a bit dodgy
though we should be fair
don't know tomorrow
as it's still not here

GOOD LUCK

Good luck is something
that you often hear
it could be farewell
if a journey near

Maybe you need it
with you when you go
it could hide a tear
that don't always show

Good luck a promise
that friends want to show
waiting at station
to hear whistle blow

THERE

Wake up and be there
be there every day
dreams made of paper
will soon blow away

Grab tight and hold me
never let me go
ours is a story
many want to know

Pure luck our meeting
right out of the blue
one glance it told me
I'm in love with you

Spent time in heaven
simply holding hands
down by the river
walked along the sands

Always together
what we did and said
our future sorted
soon after we wed

Our world fell apart
it was not to be
fate stepped between us
and took her from me

THE LINK

Memory fate and time
are linked to life's long line
part and parcel of us
will guide your life and mine

Many things like to do
and many places see
good fortune not with us
then likely not to be

We live life in stages
with many ups and downs
experience tell us
we can forget the frowns

Knowledge gained every day
sometimes what others say
keep you on the right track
never ever look back

Futures there yours alone
design it as you will
take those you love with you
their futures to full fill

LIFESPAN

Hard to find the answer
when it is time to go
hard to make decisions
and no one seems to know

A search would be useless
but many say they they know
most of it is guesswork
perhaps the truth a blow

Our life is a measure
of existence on earth
short or long some lucky
they get their moneys worth

Earth fantastic planet
we're lucky to be there
enjoy this special place
be sure to have your share

A GHOST

Heard of haunted houses
but never seen a ghost
could be I'm short sighted
and darkness hides a ghost

Found in many places
but always in the dark
often around a castle
and in the castle park

Castles seem popular
have ghosts with armour on
they make no sound at all
yet it could weigh a ton

And sometimes the ladies
clad in old fashioned wear
stroll around the castle
when full moon appear

Maybe wait for loved ones
lost in war long ago
the centuries go by
but the spirits don't go

THE SUN

Through the ages
we've worshipped the sun
and no surprise
it helps everyone
brought forth the birth
of all life on earth
a billion years
and that speck of dust
will stride to the stars
because we must
let us not forget
the special one
our one and only
glorious sun

SOFTLY

Softly, softly speak to me
hold my hand so tenderly
tell my heart what it must do
to fall in love with you

Whisper, whisper in my ear
tell me just how much you care
and would the love and joy be true
to fall in love with you

Through the years I know we'll be
always together indefinitely
fate joined us together it is true
to fall in love with you

SOMEWHERE IN MEMORY

Somewhere in memory
someone will wait for me

You ask me how I know
my heart just tells me so

The springtime that we knew
became winter for two

But time took you away
we both regret that day

For time past cannot last
together in the past

Then we did and we said
with a shake of the head

Some where dreams will come true
only there I'll find you

THE WEARY WAY

In the cycle of a life
joy and sorrow fear and strife
has its share and part to play
for all who tread the weary way

MADONNA

She stands in all her glory
with countenance divine
hers the Christmas story
Madonna of the shrine

She knows all our sorrows
our inmost secret thoughts
have faith and your tomorrows
will bring the joy you've sought

On her face unhidden
such happiness sublime
all who ask forgiven
Madonna of the shrine

THE STORY AND THE SONG

There is a story and a song
which seem to follow me
the story is of loneliness
the song of misery

And no matter how I try
to conquer all my fears
I've taught myself inside to cry
I cannot stem the tears

At the end of my story
the ending of my song
is good advice to all in love
pick well but don't pick wrong

STAIRWAY TO THE STARS

There is a stairway to the stars
which only lovers tread
each step so wonderful to feel
delight each height ahead

And all who tread this stairway
are sure to find happiness
as hand in hand they find their way
it begins with togetherness

So all you need is someone
who knows the way to the stars
who touches your heart, this is the start
of the stairway to the stars

LIFE

Life is a journey
we all have to take
from the day we are born
there is no escape
you will know
the good times
and also the bad
your life can be happy
ad also sad
so journey on
don't count the score
millions have made it
all before

OUTSIDE LOOKING IN

I often envy luckier folk
who drink together, enjoy a joke
such friendship can be hard to get
when a night is cold dark and wet
on the outside looking in

I visit dancehalls bright and gay
where many pass the time of day
yet in all this bustling throng
I am alone, join in no song
on the outside looking in

There seems a veil around my heart
which will not give me any part
of other people's happiness
its vigil keeps lest I forget
I'm outside looking in

BIRDS EYE

Sometimes I leave myself behind
to take a bird's eye view of life
through different eyes I see mankind
vision sharp as the keenest knife

Some complain they're not born free
yet they should never grumble
for there are those who cannot see
and those with minds that tumble

I see children who cannot play
with minds and bodies twisted
in beds and iron lungs they lay
why are they so afflicted

MY DAD

My dad was a soldier in the trenches
of WW1, I was there with him when
the whistle blew
and he went over
the top
no time to think
of why
you know it's bloody
do or die
bullets and shells
everywhere
the firing was heavy
as we struggled through
the mud
the bullets don't hit you
and you know they should
are we winning
just don't know
machine gun fire
again builds up
and takes a heavy toll
the morning mist is gone
then silence comes across
the front
we haven't broke through again
we slide back past
those who fell in that muddy field
and the many wounded taken
down into the trench again
for a fag and a cup of tea
home

THE VALLEY

In the valley of the doomed
a man was seen to roam
by himself he was entombed
he knew no other home

The walls were of his wishes
and promises not kept
his dreams became great fissures
past which he carefully crept

The stream which tumbled through the rocks
its very freedom to him mocks
laughing waters seemed to say
there is no other price to pay

TREAD THROUGH TIME

I tread through time and wonder why
all is dark there is no sky
just deep blue and nothing there
hard to understand or care
there could be many worlds to find
and folks like us the human kind
on every strange and distant star
and yet we find no life is there
so many things we want to share
at last my strangest journey's done
as I saw a distant sun
caressing empty worlds afar
our earth alone one special star

DELUGE

All was quiet and all was still
the sky above now overcast
then thunder roared and lightning flashed
the stygian dark abysmal

Inside the Ark the chosen few
began to praise their God on high
their faith was staunch, their hearts were true
deliverance they knew was nigh

For forty days and forty nights
the storm lashed earth spun into space
as mountain tops sank out of sight
God then forgave the human race

He made the waters cease to flow
he caused the land to reappear
bade Noah and his brethren go
and of me always walk in fear

THE CALL

If they call you go
true you can't say no
your life and family
may suffer a blow
war many heroes
and few get back home
call must be answered
and family be alone

UNEMPLOYED

On a cold wet winter's night
in a northern town
I walked in yellow gaslight
four-faced lamps cast down

A picture of dejection
I know not where to turn
for many times rejection
would not permit me earn

Each day the queue grew longer
thousands down at heel
desperate with hunger
a man will learn to steal

Yet I look around me
see things my children need
the welfare state does not ring true
when people take no heed

CHILDREN IN A DUSTY STREET

Children playing in a dusty street
their laughter gay their movement fleet
made me stand and watch a while
gave my face a wrinkled smile

They cared not for hooting cars
biting hard on chocolate bars
galloping madly to and fro
hollering loudly it's your go

It might have been myself at play
my mind went back to a distant day
when I was young and in my teens
there never were such things as jeans

Good times I had and yet I fear
for these children shed a tear
now life is lived at such a pace
an uncertain future they must face

TO SEE

The eyes have it
and no surprise
they very rarely tell you lies
the window of the soul it's said
and linked together they are wed
take you through a wonderful world
show you a rainbow just unfurled
a sunset specially on display
at dawn and dusk every day
the eye a thing of beauty too
can also show you a love that's true
the brain ensures that what it sees
is well recorded to later please
and wander down our memory lane
see all that beauty once again
your eyes will take you there and back
and memories you'll never lack
the best two friends you'll ever have
so be grateful and be glad
enjoy our wonderful world

AN OLD INN

Down a quiet country lane
I stood beside an Inn
its windows all of mullioned pane
its curtains threadbare thin

Blistered doors at crazy angles
beckoning to the last
everywhere are cobweb tangles
hiding a lurid past

And climbing up the ancient stair
which buckled shoe has trod
I feel mine host is standing there
to give a friendly nod

These walls have many a tale to tell
they've echoed loud and long
to the clash of steel when roundheads fell
for singing Cromwell's song

YOUR DREAMS

Dream your dreams
before you die
as you just
won't make it
then you'll cry
for all the things
you want to do
when life was good
and you were you
nothing any use
at all
as from the earth
you have to fall
you can't say no
so just let go
of this world
you used to know

IF YOUR BORED

If your bored
and want to try
build a ladder
to the sky
once at the top
you will recall
it's an awful
long way to fall
guess an armchair
could be quite nice
now that's a bit
of good advice

A TRIP THROUGH LIFE

Was it worth that trip through life
did you understand the strain and strife
find it easy to talk to some
or do others leave you on the run
why do people go to war?
to win a fight or settle a score
many things to see and do
of course they may not all be you
friends and neighbours can be good
and then again they could draw blood
can't always turn the other cheek
they might think that you're a freak
so do battle if you must
you won't find everybody just
to travel your road the only way
it can be different every day
good and bad are sorted out
and in the end you'll have no doubt
your trip through life shows each new day
so many things so differently
give and take as best you can
as life on earth you try to span
I think it's getting rather late
I see St. Peter at the gate
and yes as usual I am late

WHY

To fall in love is very strange
and find that someone cares
who you are and what you are
in many different ways
her eyes of blue
her beauty too
can hold you in its spell
you're holding hands together
and sort of in a daze
we cuddle close and whisper
that these are happy days
I want to understand it
but shouldn't really try
fate brought us together
and we'll never ask it why

ECHO

There's an echo in the valley
where we wandered long ago
and it tells me you remember
how I begged you not to go
how I pleaded how I needed
you so constantly
will it always be an echo
or will you come back to me
then you'll hold me
then you'll kiss me
and you'll love me tenderly
say you'll never ever leave me
let it echo endlessly

ALLAN AND JEAN

If you should come looking for Allan and Jean
you'll find them together like they've always been
no one could part them though many tried
so great was their love, together they died
they were so happy they were so young
their last dying wish that the bells should be rung
many folks pointed and many folks stared
when they were together many folks sneered
they only left high school shortly before
then they found love and asked nothing more
they were so happy they were so young
their last dying wish that the bells should be rung
they wanted to marry, their parents said no
you both have a very long time to go
stop seeing each other then you'll be sure
and both understand whats love's really for
they were so happy they were so young
their last dying wish that the bells should be rung
they ran off together happy and gay
how could they know this was their last day
and fell from the cliffs that run by the shore
they found each other as never before
they were so happy they were so young
their last dying wish that the bells should be rung

ESCAPE

To dream is to break
all the rules
and for a while
join all the fools
worries you have put away
leave them for another day
spread your wings leave you behind
your other self seeking the quiet kind
of places there are by the score
like walking on a sandy shore
of deserts that run by the sea
South Africa's skeleton coast I see
as Egypt's pyramids pierce the sky
high above we travel by
flamingos rise and meet the sun
a beautiful sight for everyone
so back to earth we make our way
myself and me enjoyed the day
it's just a way to get away

TREASURE YOUR MEMORIES

Memories are your treasure
maybe your only gold
special secret hidden
for only you to hold
no one can destroy them
or let them fade away
they are yours forever
as fresh as yesterday

CORRIDOR OF TIME

Down the corridor of time
through the rain
and through the shine
your love and laughter
calls to me
echoing my name
when will I find you
where will you be
I've searched the heavens
and questioned the sea

Why are you hiding
so far away from me
the North Star sparkles
maybe it knows
I hear your laughter
when the east wind blows
it echoes and echoes
are you lost in space
on some distant star
I will love you forever
wherever you are

NIGHT SKY

At night I looked into the sky
and watched a brilliant star go by
and wondered why the earth was so
wondered where the star would go
So many tiny points of light
millions more beyond my sight
I found it hard to understand
that man himself was very grand
the world itself so very small
our universe a tiny ball

AN OLD MAN

He was old by many years
his grandchild round him ran
and brought a twinkle to his eye
as only children can

He'd been in two or three wars
had medals in his trunk
and wished he'd had a penny for
the times when he'd been drunk

He seen most corners of the world
and sailed the seven seas
and seen a good few flags unfurled
In a following breeze

Of good times he's had his share
he's had his slice of life
content to fill and old armchair
with memories and pipe

JUST A CLOCK

Tick tock
just a clock
nothing special
nothing fine
just a way
to tell the time
high on the mantel
hard to see
time doesn't matter
when youre three
the hands go round
and never stop
as long as someone
winds the clock
it travels with you
through the years
hears the laughter
sees the tears
when at last
we've all left home
he's still there ticking
all alone
just a clock

LIFE THOUGHTS

To have a heart and mind at ease
to savour joy, these qualities
cannot be found upon the ground
but only on life's troubled seas

A TIME TO

A time to live
a time to die
a time to laugh
a time to cry
a time to think
a time to dream
a time to remember
the life you've seen
to get it right
or get it wrong
the trip through the years
was never long
a time to love
a time of tears
so travel your road
and look round the bend
you'll find it's been worth it
right through to the end

FATE IS THE FUTURE

We all have a future
if fate grants us one
by that special Son
who knows all the answers
understands all the fears
well known to us all
for two thousand years

THE SEARCH

And he went forth but could not find
the light he knew which was so kind
which gave the very soul its glow
and lit two thousand years ago

He left the places he knew well
to search in lands where strangers dwell
ever faithful ever sure
that it may lie on a foreign shore

He climbed the mountains scoured the hills
and looked in heaven's window sills
even the oceans could not tell
of the golden light that fell

In many years he journeyed far
his search for this especial star
had robbed him of his health and youth
brought him at last the awful truth

That no singular ray is there
the light of God is everywhere
and all who seek have but to ask
Him in their hearts to share His task

RHYME

You don't need a reason
nor any special time
to put your thoughts together
and try to make them rhyme

Write about the good times
write about the bad
make your reader happy
or make him very sad

Take him to the country
take him to the town
make him wear the longest face
or be happy like a clown

You don't need a reason
or any special time
to put your thoughts together
and try to make them rhyme

A ROSE

To find a rose in a concrete street
to feel the world is at your feet
how can one be convention wise
looking into the rear strained eyes
of a young girl seeking love
away together hand in hand
is there need for a golden hand
young hearts in love can do no wrong
and parting's never thought of

WALES

Mountains valleys woods and vales
this is the scenery which is Wales
Castles of granite standing still
Roman legions could not kill
the spirit which is Wales
land of song and many voices
they're close to God and He rejoices
His blessing gives to one and all
as evening bells of chapel call
The spirit which is Wales

SUNDOWN

Sundown on the prairie
another day is through
night comes creeping up on me
disturbing thoughts of you

By my lonely campfire
I sit and watch the flames
leaping high up to the sky
whispering your name

Those great big stars keep twinkling
I think they know I care
but how can I stop thinking
of the love I couldn't share

THE BOMB

It seems we've reached the climax
the ultimate in fear
mankind should be in mourning
for this Godforsaken era

Each nation at the ready now
the well selected few
planning annihilation
of all that lived and grew

Our scientists can tell us
how best to tear asunder
will generations yet to come
deformed forgive this blunder

ETERNAL LOVE

Alone am I
searching through a dark night sky
never were the stars so high
shining eerily

Come to me
touch my lips so tenderly
you alone the key

Take my hand
lead me in this timeless land
such happiness I understand
love me eternally

JUNGLE DRUMS

Drums in the night
echoing my heart
where is daylight
long we apart

Moonlight through the trees
jasmine in the breeze
these things I love
these things I need

Will you return
my heart never learn
those jungle drums
have me heartbroken

CAN'T SAY

I can't say how much I love you
I can't say how much I care
one day I'll speak of these things
when no one can overhear

Light a candle at the altar
and for me say a prayer
speak to Him and ask forgiveness
I will understand the tears

Please don't ask me of the future
as it's so far away
just a glimmer in the darkness
which surrounds me every day

DEREHAM DOWN

In the valley of Dereham Down
once a busy cotton town
now the mills no longer hum
to feed the worker from the slum
prosperity has fled

The cobbled streets are sprouting grass
that echoed clogs to morning mass
no laughter at the local Inn
no tankard frothing at the brim
a ghost town of the dead

Deserted streets and alleyways
so hard to picture market days
all so quiet all so still
even the wind has time to kill
and rustles leaves of red

Factory chimneys rearing high
like angry fingers to the sky
and pointing state accusingly
why have my people gone from me
and give me up for dead

ARE WE ALONE?

This is the time
this is the place
meet the universe
face to face

And ask it how
it got so far
and what exactly
is a star?

And how the Earth
has come to be
a solo world
infinitely

Countless planets
gleam in space
yet are we alone
the human race

SEARCHING MY STAR

Been a long time searching
everywhere I go
and even if I find it
I'll never really know
did I get the answer
or am I still in doubt
will her light surround me
or will it cast me out
can such a small and tiny star
spread its brilliance from afar
and make my wish come true

SHADOWS

Of all the corners of the earth
and all the seven seas
nothing gives me greater pleasure
than a chair to take my ease

And to watch the firelight shadows
flickering on the wall
then fancy sets me dreaming
of things beyond recall

About the folks who lived here
what they did and said
and if the ones who passed away
come back from the dead

To search for long lost loved ones
the well remembered places
where they played in carefree youth
with happy smiling faces

Flitting through the galleries
no sound disturbs the air
as many silent ghostly feet
tread the wide old oaken stair

OUR DREAMS

Do you recall
you came to me last fall
when the leaves had turned to brown

Then you I saw
my heart could not withdraw
knowing love at last I'd found

All the world stood still
you held me tight
vowing to fulfill

The dreams we had that night
and yet I find
that fate can be unkind

I walk alone once more
for you are gone
those dreams we counted on

THE ROVER

What is it that makes me roam
directs my steps away from home
ever onward ever sure
of sights I've never seen before

And people whom I've never met
and perhaps will soon forget
nevertheless I journey on
as though hunted on the run

In search of that I know not what
could be itchy feet I've got
so many places I've not been
so many faces I've not seen

When at last I've settled down
in some quiet country town
you'll find me in the local bar
yarning of those lands afar

HAPPY DAYS

Happy days
come and go
can't take time off
boss said no
he said good cheer
after Christmas
and in New Year

STARRY NIGHT

As evening merges into night
the stars of the universe clear and bright
reveal themselves in the darkening sky
and shine like lanterns to light the passerby

Over the hills glides a crescent moon
down in the woods hear a nightingale croon
the hills and the valleys lay bathed in wan light
as the pale yellow moon looks down from her height

From among the trees comes the eerie cry
of the wise old owl as he wings his way by
up in the heavens stars gleam still
as the moon dips over a distant hill

THE END

I was there when all was lost
I helped the Gods to count the cost
when from the earth all life was tossed
this man's final blunder

I saw a world torn from the skies
and heard a million anguished cries
alas their voices could not rise
above such earthbound thunder

And now at last there's naught to see
the very dust infinity
the Gods gaze hard and angrily
but even they must wonder

CURIOSITY

I often wonder what life's for
the reason why or is there more
than meets the eye of the average man
can he discover in life's short span
the answer to the universe
the way dumb animals converse
what is wrong and what is right
the exact formula and source of light
wise old men in ages past
they studied hard and came at last
in deliberations did they find
that it would take a master mind
one man's brain could ill afford
all these wonders to absorb
and still retain a level head
and not end up in a hospital bed
to rant and rave of glories past
maybe an arm in a plaster cast
on his card you'll see don't touch
here lies a man who knew too much

OLD FOLKS HOME

All around are faces
and stories they can tell
for these are all the old folks
their age and echoing bell

They talk about their loved ones
and how for them they cared
but very few are visited
by the families they reared

YOU ARE MY WORLD

You are my world
my one desire
life without you
would be flame without fire
you are the beginning
and end for me
not just tomorrow
but through all eternity
yet fate brought you to me
and strange as it seems
I knew you would be waiting
because I believe in dreams
now as I hold you
surely loneliness is past
my anxious heart trembles
to know our love will last
and with the passing
of each and every day
I will learn to love you more
in each and every way

NEVER FOREVER

Never forever
she's no longer there
promises broken
just memories to share

Never forever
will she hold me tight
kiss and caress me
all through the night

And now whenever
the tears start to fall
my heart will remember
love beyond recall

HAPPY B DAY

Open one eye look around
must be in an ozzy I'll be bound
white and polished funny smells
now and then I can hear yells
funny sounds and funny voices
I can't move so got no choices
been in the dark so very long
find these bright lights rather strong
think this world's a busy place
yet all the nurses work with grace
roll on sleep what can I say
I only got here yesterday

SHE

And yet I find
on looking round
there's naught to see
that once was me
no memory
however kind
can I be sure
which way to go
the night is dark
no light or spark
my heart this part
alone is pure
and free from sin
which I know well
all Satan's ways
I spent my days
so in a daze
so far from Him
the lonely years
till she came by
she took my hand
she understands
God's promised land
a time for tears

GAZE

Take time off from your troubles
leave them here on the ground
and raise your eyes up to clear blue skies
where tranquillity can be found

When things don't go the way they should
and you can't see your way through the maze
it's as well to recall some would give their all
just to stand in the sunset and gaze

When you don't know the way and your future's in doubt
and your dreams are no longer secure
have faith in your heart to make a new start
and to find a path which is sure

CALL ME

Call me and I'll come
crook your finder and I'll run
if you give me just one wintery smile
I'd run a mile
call me and I'll come

Whisper and I'll hear
you don't know how much I care
I want to hold you tenderly
closely to me
whisper and I'll hear

Love me and you'll know
I could never let you go
you have set my world on fire
with one desire
love me and you'll know

A HAUNTED HEART

A haunted heart
can't leave you behind
why is love so unkind?
why does it make us so blind?

We'll never know
what kind of life we'd have led
so many things unsaid
unopened letters unread

I wish I'd tried
more to understand you
forgive me if I'm blue
I can't help loving you

Is it too late
just one more chance a start
painful being apart
empty place in my heart

ALONE WITH YOU

I think of you at daybreak
with the rising of the sun
you're still there when it's setting
and another day is done
alone with you

I think of you in the evening
when the starry sky at night
sparkling with brilliance
sheds its pale and gentle light
alone with you

I think of you each moment
just wishing you were here
for there are many, many thoughts
I could whisper in your ear
alone with you

JUST JEAN

Eyes of blue
hair of gold
never in your heart to scold
Just Jean

Sweet sixteen
never a care
such fantastic love to share
Just Jean

Nothing special
smiles with ease
we hold hands tightly just to please
Just Jean

Always together
never apart
first time we met she stole my heart
Just Jean

Alas fate came
and crossed our tracks
so never again will she join her Max
Just Jean

LET IT BE

Hear me and say you care
this is the once in a lifetime
no other time is the right time
let it be so from now on

Love is like a journey
once started you must carry on
sometimes if you're lucky
you might find she's the one

Tell me you need me near
as I put my arms around you
say that you're glad I found you
let it be so from now on

LEGION OF THE DAMNED

There is a legion called the damned
who tread the midnight hour
between heaven and earth they stand
dimension number four

No beginning to their week
no end to their year
the sanctity of the soul they seek
both good and evil fear

And down the corridor of time
they must forever tread
waiting for the heavenly sign
when God will raise his dead

WANDERLUST

To wander slowly on the sands
or stare across the sea
the winds can whisper of lands
where I would rather be

Roaming through the streets of Cadiz
where the wild flamencos danced
on the caravan to Mecca
penance for a green kufi

Sees Himalayan sunset
lost in snow white crispen world
this is the forbidden Tibet
where many spinning prayer wheels curled

To stride along the wall of China
where blood of Mongol warriors ran
and the hordes of all the Tartars
fought to the death with Genghis Khan

To wander slowly on the sands
or stare across the sea
the winds can whisper of many lands
where I would rather be

SPACE

I wander through the heavens
like a ghost in search of God
where can she have got to
I find it very odd

Each galaxy so distant
and very very far
yet nevertheless I search for her
on every single star

I know she'll search for beauty
and fantastic colours there
outer space a dream come true
for a traveller like her

One day I will find her
and without a word to say
we'll kiss and stay together
for every single day

New worlds are very special
we'll seek them hand in hand
just one fantastic future
we both can understand

REACH FOR THE STARS

Reach for the stars
and find your way home
that's where we came from
and never alone
we are part of the planets
and more distant worlds
and put together
as universe unfurls
in deep dark space
where no suns shine
we streak through the cosmos
for aeons of time
until our legendary birth
on the tiny tiny planet earth

OLD AGE MEMORIES

There comes a time for everyone
when we have had our day
when hands are gnarled and withered
and our hair has turned to grey

There comes a time for memories
when eyes no longer see
to wander far down memory lane
where happiness can be

There comes a time for leaving
this world we know so well
but death will wait for no one
and who is there to tell

IN A CHURCHYARD

Not asleep nor yet awake
I had the strangest dream
that I was in a churchyard
and on a stone did lean
on reading the inscription
I found that Captain Crewe
a grand old seaman of the line
had died 1802
I wondered what he'd looked like
what commands he'd had
and if he'd been around the Horn
when the weather had been bad
there on another stone quite clear
for all the world to see
God had taken Pamela Jane
a little girl of three
these and many more I read of
history in stone pages
it seemed death cared not when he called
so varied were the ages
deep in thought I gave a start
an old man touched my hand
leading me back through the gate said
don't try to understand

A VISION

In the quiet of the night
I saw a vision gleaming white
the figure of a woman there
all in white knelt in prayer
up she rose and beckoned me
with a bony finger follow me
we climbed the stair to a lumber room
bathed in the light of a pale yellow moon
the spirit moved from place to place
such desperation on a pale young face
she screamed and cried but no sound came
the agony of a ghost in pain
then she was gone I stood alone
amidst the rubbish of a home
next day I cleared the attic through
and rotten boards replaced with new
there enshrined in the grime of years
the skeleton of a child appears

BEGGARS CUP

Never pass a beggar
you see in the street
may you'll be there
and on that same seat
time and tide
could wash you up
and it's your turn
to hold the beggars cup

GEISHA GIRL

Fragrant lotus blossoms
decorate her hair
almond eyes hold mild surprise
my eastern lady fair

Hers a gentle nature
slender lovely hands
speak to me so delicately
I can understand

She bows at each meeting
welcoming you there
precious pearl this Geisha girl
my eastern lady fair

CLIMB TOGETHER

To climb the highest mountain
is nought by far
to look in heaven's windows
and find a star
to roam the wide world over
I'll search for thee
I'd just go on forever
indefinitely
I know some day
I'll find you
of that I'm sure
though not so far away
or on some foreign shore
then we'll be together
forever ever more

VALERIE

A girl so full of fun and life
she could and did run rings around me
auburn hair and emerald eyes
a lovely smile that could surprise
Valerie

You could take her anywhere
her lovely figure made some stare
she'd flash a smile and never care
proud to be
Valerie

Often wondered since we met
just how lucky can you get
she'd shake her head and hold me tight
this was to be our last goodnight
Valerie

When they came and took her away
all they said was better this way
where she's gone they would not say
lost am I without her
Valerie

DOWN MEMORY LANE

Can I go down memory lane
and hold hands with the past
turn the pages and be
a much younger me?
many things I'd like to see
many places I'd like to be
but little things I do recall
are climbing over a backyard wall
seeking empty jam jars
two would get you a cinema seat
every Saturday morn
pocket money never had
so jam jars were the norm
those jam jars helped
to make my day
down memory lane
on Saturday

PINNACLE OF PERFECTION

Part and parcel of our lives
is love and hope affection
yet so many fail to reach
that pinnacle perfection
for the perfect man must never err
in any of his days
and consequently spends his life
avoiding pleasant ways

THE EYES DECIDE

The eyes can tell you
yes or no
the eyes can tell you
come or go
the eyes can show you
love and care
and can tell you
to beware
they have their glances
stored away
always ready for display
for friends it means
a special glance
for others you can
take a chance
the eyes will never
miss a thing
and photograph your world

A LITTLE GIRL

Think of something pink and blue
a touch of gold a delicate hue
of pristine white a shaft of light
a mass of hair with eyes so bright
this is a little girl

She's all these things and many more
at evening time she's near the door
listening hard for daddy's knock
one eye fixed upon the clock
impatient little girl

At bedtime she's up the stairs
Daddy's hand held tight in hers
he'll tell her stories quell her fears
and brush away her little cares
just Daddy's little girl

THE MERMAID

Her smile was gentle to behold
such sweet red lips could never scold
or so the sailors story told
down beneath the sea

Her hair was long and golden too
her breasts were fine and in full view
with eyes that were so very blue
down beneath the sea

She made her home among the reefs
and sang her song of watery deeps
of how the ocean takes and keeps
down beneath the sea

The lookout was the first to see
this beauty rise from out the sea
and like a man dived gallantry
down beneath the sea

His ship sped onward into shoals
her bow was torn with gaping holes
so perished eighty honest souls
down beneath the sea

HAVE TIME

We all have time
or have we
some will spend it wisely
one day at a time
so how are we to know
could we use it better
or just have a blow
seconds often save a life
can also lose one too
time you've lots of
when you're young
and more when you get old
the summer seems much warmer
and the winter very cold
so time must watch the weather
and tell us what to do
to wrap up warm in winter
keep cool in summer too

THE STRANGER

I saw a stranger raise his eyes
above this world to sunlit skies
he gazed around for what he knew
was in this wonderland of blue
for here no sound disturbs the air
no unhappiness or care
could ever find a resting place
could ever crease the stranger's face
this was a man who knew the world
and one whom cruel fate had hurled
into the melting pot of life
to fight a long and bitter fight
yet even he forgets such things
for a little while his heart has wings
and understands serenity
and contemplates eternity

STAR SEARCH

The strangest girl I ever met
was searching for a star
it seemed unreal for one so young
her thoughts to stray so far
yet when I got to know her well
and looked into her eyes
I saw a perfect picture there
reflecting starry skies
she said she needed someone
like a house would need a wall
someone she could come to
when her castles began to fall
I loved her then and gently touched
her soft and curling hair
and held her close and whispered things
that only she could hear
she said she sought contentment
not so difficult to find
if you can love and be loved
you will have a peaceful mind
her hand stretched out
but could not touch
the star contentment
that meant so much
it broke my heart
to see her strive
and hear her sob
like a child of five
to comfort there is no way
little I can do or say
I can only join her heart in flight
towards her star on a thoughtful night

THE PAST

I think the past
best place to be
all you need
is memory
see those
you loved and lost
and things you did
with fingers crossed
see places known
no longer there
and meet that girl
with golden hair
all gone
but can be seen
every time
I have a dream

THE DENIAL

The man who climbed the mountain
to look in God's right eye
was eager to discover
a deity to deny

And at the top most spur of rock
he stood and he beheld
the misdemeanours of his life
in sin he had excelled

He could not ask forgiveness
for of Him he knew not
in desperation flung himself
into he knew not what

'Twas God alone who saw him fall
who watched his body roll
who came and stood beside it
to lead away his soul

THOUGHTS OF LIFE

Sometimes I stand and look at life
see all the worry toil and strife
which tears a heart asunder
and wonder if it's really worth
taking part in another's birth
for they also will wonder

NATIONS

In the silence of the night
I had the strangest dream
that God had asked me to unite
the nations for His theme

To stop the murder and the strife
to end the endless grief
to throw away the bloodstained knife
and find a peace to keep

To help his people understand
each other's different ways
and show them that the promised land
was well within their gaze

So enormous was the task
it weighed upon my mind
and yet the question should be asked
how could I save mankind?

I called the leaders to my side
and asked them if they knew
of rules by which they could abide
to which they could be true

Each one gave his version
of what had best be done
but no one knew for certain
or trusted anyone

They argued back and forth at length
I gave up in despair
it seems mankind will never learn
to treat his neighbours fair

THE NUN

Listen surely you can hear
the tolling of a convent bell
stealing through the cold night air
on my ears it strangely fell

All around the snow lay deep
the convent wall forbidding high
like sentinels who never sleep
solid stone under leaden sky

With eager fingers up I climbed
for in my heart I knew I'd see
the reason why the bell had chimed
to herald the nativity

Through stained glass windows candle lit
I saw the holy knelt in prayer
praising God with fingers knit
as with one voice a heavenly choir

GIRLS GIRLS GIRLS

Very often laughing
and sometimes hear them cry
can be good pals
always keep us guessing
and hard to understand
most end up as mothers
then their hands are full
and on the river of life
the next generation they float

CHISHOLM TRAIL

I'll pin my star on a new horizon
I'll set my hopes on a different scene
and look around for a brand new sunset
and look around for a brand new dream

Where coyotes wail on the Chisholm trail
and the stars hang high in a cloudless sky
where the rivers sing and valleys wander
and the wind tells tales of a time gone by

I'll turn my back on a world that's angry
I'll turn my back on a love that's lost
and hide my tears on a lonely hillside
and hide my heart till the pain is past

Don't look for me as I'll be long gone
a silhouette in the setting sun
a lonely trail that I must wander
a lonely heart that loved and lost

IN SEARCH OF TOMORROW

I'll go in search of tomorrow
In spite of what they say
for I believe in tomorrow
another chance another day

I'll stride into the sunset
I'll reach up for the sky
leave this world far behind me
till I can find my sweet by and by

My world was so full of sorrows
my world was so full of tears
my world could give me no laughter
or teach me to smile, such long lonely years

I know some day I'll find you
I know somehow you'll be there
I know if I keep searching
one day I'll find my beautiful dream

THE SEA CALLS ME

Standing on these cliffs I find
the sea can tranquillize the mind
the rolling combers ever roar
a battered windswept rocky shore

The seabirds send their strident call
yet through the noise peace overall
these green depths full of mystery
forever calling out to me

THE THEME

A melody so strange and haunting
kept running through my mind and taunting
throughout the day throughout the night
I knew such happiness deep delight
my heart would rise with the rising theme
high in the sky to some cloudy scene
my song would echo from star to star
till all the universe near and far
in one accord would join with me
and make their plea for liberty
to spin off in perpetual night
away from the sun's caressing light
the music reached crescendo now
I thought the gods would take their bow
and grudgingly give up the key
unlock mankind's real destiny

I WONDER

I wonder if they'll miss me
when I am dead and gone
and seen the last of this world
to seek the other one

I wonder if they'll miss me
down at the local Inn
and will my glass still be there
in case I'm coming in

I wonder if they'll miss me
whose arms have held me tight
who shared with me the good times
and shared my bed at night

I wonder if they'll miss me
those friends so good and true
will they remember times gone by
and shed a tear or two

WE COME AND GO

You miss people
and when they go
then it's your turn
to leave also
this is the way
our life goes round
seems all of us
cemetery bound

A TRIP GOODBYE

Say goodbye to body
and say goodbye to time
say goodbye to all things
the end of my lifetime

Leave this world behind me
summer and winter too
weather just don't matter
and all I liked to do

Knew I'd have to travel
knew I'd have to go
it's a trip we all take
to nowhere that I know

THREE LITTLE LETTERS

Why just three little letters?
why it can mean so much?
why it can remind me
of your gentle touch?

When will we be together?
when will I hold you tight?
when will it be forever
in your arms every night?

How can I show that I love you?
how can I show that I care?
how can my arms surround you
when only a dream is there?

WANDERER

Wanderer wanderer
why do you roam
can't you settle
have you no home
or are you still searching
for the special One
that you knew in the past
and now long gone
time is a healer
or so people say
but can also take people
and memories away
so stay with the present
forget yesterday
we don't live forever
so use everyday

DREAM

It's as easy
as I say
half asleep
the best way
you can put it
to the test and
have a very
comfy rest
good things recalled
at the top
bad things just
forget the lot
settle down and
you can say
I just don't know
a better way
don't even have
to pay
to dream your troubles away

BEAUTY IS NOT FOREVER

Beauty is not forever
time can take it away
and leave only wrinkles
with hair that's turning grey
but we can all recall the good times
from memories that last
an open door that can explore
happiness in the past

WISHES

I often wish that I could fly
and leave this troubled world
to spread my wings in a darkened sky
where the Milky Way is curled
and see the starlet clusters
like gems on nature's brow
for a millions year their lustre
was brilliant then and now

STAR GIRL

Long ago
through the mist of time
I lost my lover
who was always mine
she was so different
surrounded by stars
commanding the planets
a leader on Mars
often in orbit
a galaxy queen
an incredible person
a star spangled dream
maybe I'll find her
for time is my friend
then together forever
a fantastic end

BEYOND

Look beyond tomorrow
what is there to see
is it wise to seek it
there could be tragedy
many people plan ahead
while others have the fear
will they be around to see it
or no longer here
gypsies tell your future
some of them quite old
fate may tell you when to go
usually you never know
when you've got to go, you go

COURAGE

Sometimes you must lead
and others will follow
sometimes you must fight
and others will fall
life has a worth and a value
and for love you
would give your all
who knows how to answer
who knows if there's a call
just have the guts to lead them
have the guts to fall
are you doing the right thing
with your back against the wall?
go out there to win it
always answer the call
lead and they will follow
they will give their all

ANGIE

Gentle quiet hard to know
eyes that tell you yes or no
a smile that spreads across her face
she looks and is so full of grace

You look at her and then you find
that this girl is a special kind
can take you to a world unknown
with one sentence on her phone

A golden girl that sees her world
in someone's arms so tightly curled
such love and care to give away
I hope that Angie's here to stay

JEWELS IN THE RAIN

Jewels in the rain
sparkling my name
life will never be the same
without you

Do you have to stray
and be so far away
I can't face another day
without you

My jewels in the rain
please speak to me again
fate says I will remain
without you

TURNING GREY

It might be old
it might be gold
is turning grey
the bouncing locks
no longer on display
those sparkling eyes
full of surprise
I remember to this day
but time can give us
memories
that are never ever past
an open door to
yesterday
that will forever last

HEAVEN

Don't look for heaven
you'll find it here on earth
and if you fall off into space
you could find it
a most unpleasant place
please do not jump too hard
or you'll be flitting around
a considerable distance off the ground
but gravity has this special glue
to stop us floating into the blue
we have a satellites very high
two hundred and fifty miles in the sky
it guides us on the earth below
tells us when the high winds blow
gravity will keep us safe on earth
and our spy in the sky of priceless worth

DOING TIME

Doing time
stand in line
the good times gone
so goodbye sun
early to bed
and not well fed

Doing time
stand in line
proud of her
a dream come true
in my small cell
it can't be true

Doing time
stand in line
too much time
to think of her
fantastic eyes
and golden hair

Doing time
stand in line
sometimes I sigh
when dawn arrives
how I'd welcome
sunny skies

Doing time
stand in line
wonder when
we'll meet again
doors are locked

A rattled chain
an officer bellows
the old refrain
you're doing time
stand in line

LOVE

Gently gently
hold my hand
help my heart
to understand
the love and care
I have for you
is so tender
is so true
always always
hold me tight
cling to me
all through
the night
never ever
let me go
I'm so lucky
to love you so
never ever
say goodbye
together forever
until we die

A GAMBLE

You fight the good fight
with all your might
and never ever win
the only peace and quiet you get
is the grave they drop you in

RELAX

To have
and to hold
to let life
unfold
is everyone's
wish and desire
but life's subject
to
the time you
go through
a good time
before you
retire

THE PAST

I think the past
best place to be
all you need
is memory
see those
you loved and lost
and things you did
with fingers crossed
see places known
no longer there
and meet that girl
with golden hair
all gone
but can be seen
every time
I have a dream

YOU CAN ASK

You can ask all
the questions
break all the rules
think like a
wise man
or ponder like fools
no one has
solved it
information we lack
and after they
die
none ever come
back
one man
knows
and travels
the earth
sometimes seeking
his place of birth

He's seen all
the battles
agony and strife
as his people
kill each other
destroying life
will it change
he shakes his head
even my name
is used in vain
again and again
yet he stands alone
and watches hoping
we'll change our ways
sees the earth
as our mother
and a dawn of
better days

JOURNEY OF DREAMS

If your dreams go that far
you could journey to a star
see the planets on your list
and settle down on one that fits
they can be different than our earth
depends on what you think they're worth
something that you need to know
nobody there to say hello
some have sunshine day and night
so at bedtime draw the curtain tight
Mars has lots of stony plain
your search for water could be in vain
nights very cold, days very hot
then again it's worth
going back to good old earth
nothing very scary there
just a tiny little sphere

A ROUGH DIAMOND

A rough diamond
hard to recognize
looks a bit scruffy
looks a bit odd
unlikely to be worth much
value very low
it's got to be polished
to sparkle and to glow
a rough diamond
you can meet them every day
not much conversation
not a lot to say
been in many places
but never ever stay
good to have them with you
they've travelled many ways
rough diamonds hard to find
but if and when you do
you'll never have
a better friend
to stand alongside you

RACE TIME AND SPACE

Are time and space
having a race
to find who's leader
in this place?
to be the first
and may be cursed
that pulled the worlds
asunder
forced the galaxies
far apart this one
fantastic start
we would
all remember
Jupiter
Uranus too
would make tracks
for somewhere new
our tiny earth
forgotten too
as having heavens
settle down
we find a brilliant
dawn is born

SILVER AND GOLD

Someday one day
we'll walk hand in hand
together as ever
to our promised land
where the sun
shines by day
and moon by night
sparkles your eyes
what a beautiful sight
a world to explore
we could go there
and always be sure
new memories to learn
a new life to see
a fantastic future
for you and for me
our sunlight
and moonlight
will always be free
silver and gold
for you and for me

SLEEP

To sleep is to avoid all care
even the light of day won't dare
to wake us from much needed rest
our heads against the pillow pressed
to dream there'll come another day
when better times have come to stay

ONE DAY

I think one day
I'll find my way
to meet the perfect girl

I know she's there
I saw the tear
my thoughts were in a whirl

I saw blue eyes
a big surprise
but was that smile for me

We're bound to meet
in any street
and pretty scared I'll be

If she walked past
and did not ask
are you looking for me

My dream would die
I'd give a sigh
not get bye without you

MR ELS

Kept hearing bells
a ringing in his head
he said I think if this keeps up
I'll have to go to bed
the doctor came and said the thought
the problem hard to see
and added if you've any left
I'll have a drop with thee

THE TOAD

I met a toad
in London road
as busy as a bee
and stood a while
and watched him
singing merrily
he didn't seem to worry
didn't seem to care
and soon a crowd had gathered
to give the toad a cheer
I never knew that toads could sing
but now I'm pretty sure
my ears have not recovered
they are very very sore

ANGUS MACBRIDE

Angus MacBride
could never abide
fish on his table for tea
'tis known he once said
I'd rather be dead
than have fynnon
aswimmin in me

JIM MCFALL

I knew a man called Jim McFall
who wouldn't eat no bread at all
the sight of butties turned him green
he with a loaf was never seen
and to this day he's just the same
the bakers can't abide his name
and if they see him walking by
all the stale cakes at him shy

ABOUT THE AUTHOR

Born and bred in the back streets of Liverpool and still turned up at the publishers desk. I guess I must be lucky, my mum rented a house in Garden Street, Liverpool on the edge of town. Dad was injured in the 1914-1918 war and was paralysed down the right side of his body. He got nine shillings a week war pension and my mum got a pound from the Public Assistance.

My dad died in February 1941 just before my twelfth birthday. My oldest brother was 20 and fighting in Burma, my other two sisters were 15 and 17.

At 18 I was called up for the National Service and joined the RAF. By this time I had only written one poem, life was tough and jobs were hard to find but we did our best. In the 60's I got married and had two children.

We emigrated to South Africa in the early 70s and had another child. We spent 13 years travelling around Africa following the jobs between South Africa, Rhodesia/Zimbabwe before returning back to the Wales in 1985. I did a few creative writing jobs while I was in Africa but this was more as a hobby than a career. I was 55 when we returned to the UK, jobs was hard to find especially at my age. We then moved to Daventry in 1986 as there were better job prospects, this helped provide some extra pocket money.

With more time on my hands I started to write more and have had many poems published in various books. This has inspired me to write my own books.